BATTLEGROUND AMERICA

CEMETERY HILL

BATTLEGROUND AMERICA GUIDES offer a unique approach to the battles and battlefields of America. Each book in the series highlights a small American battlefield—sometimes a small portion of a much larger battlefield. All of the units, important individuals, and actions of each engagement on the battlefield are described in a clear and concise narrative. Historical images and modern-day photographs tie the dramatic events of the past to today's battlefield site and highlight the importance of terrain in battle. The present-day battlefield is described in detail with suggestions for touring the site.

BATTLEGROUND AMERICA

CEMETERY HILL

The Struggle for the High Ground, July 1–3, 1863

Terry L. Jones

DA CAPO PRESS
A Member of the Perseus Books Group

Da Capo Press
A Member of the Perseus Books Group

Photos courtesy of: U.S. Army Military History Institute—12,
16, 19, 27, 28, 30, 31, 45, 46, 48, 51 (bottom), 54, 73, 82, 84, 85,
108, 110; National Archives—17, 24, 34 (top and right), 36, 44,
58, 67; Library of Congress—10, 34 (bottom), 42, 86, 88, 92, 95;
Gettysburg National Military Park—51 (top), 71, 74, 81;
Civil War Library and Museum—26.

Maps by Theodore P. Savas

Cataloging-in-Publication data for this book is available from
the Library of Congress.

ISBN 0–306–81235–5
Published by Da Capo Press
A Member of the Perseus Books Group
http://www.dacapopress.com

Da Capo Press books are available at special discounts for bulk
purchases in the U.S. by corporations, institutions, and other
organizations. For more information, please contact the Special
Markets Department at the Perseus Books Group, 11 Cambridge
Center, Cambridge, MA 02142, or call (800) 255-1514 or
(617) 252–5298, or e-mail j.mccrary@perseusbooks.com.

1 2 3 4 5 6 7 8 9—05 04 03

For Danny and Larry,
my brothers and fellow history buffs

ACKNOWLEDGMENTS

In preparing this volume on Cemetery Hill, the author was greatly assisted by not only the park personnel at the Gettysburg National Military Park, but also the kind citizens of Gettysburg, who were helpful in pointing out the numerous roads and streets. Also, series editor Ted Savas was his usual good-natured self and greatly enhanced the work with his insight, expertise, and fine maps. Finally, I would like to express my heartfelt gratitude to my wife, Carol, and daughters, Laura and Amie, for their support.

CONTENTS

INTRODUCTION

IN JUNE 1863, GENERAL ROBERT E. LEE and his Confederate Army of Northern Virginia held the initiative in Virginia after defeating Major General Joseph Hooker's Army of the Potomac at the Battle of Chancellorsville in May. Lee decided to invade Pennsylvania that summer to take the war out of Virginia and to gather supplies in rich Pennsylvania. The capture of a major city or a great battlefield victory on the enemy's soil might also strengthen the growing peace movement in the North and perhaps finally win the Confederacy foreign recognition. Although President Jefferson Davis preferred a more defensive strategy, he had confidence in Lee's judgment and approved the invasion.

After first clearing the Federals from Virginia's Shenandoah Valley, Lee entered Pennsylvania in mid-June with about 75,000 men. During this move, one of the campaign's major controversies began unfolding when he allowed Major General J. E. B. Stuart to take the bulk of the cavalry on a raid. Stuart had been surprised by the enemy cavalry in the Battle of Brandy Station in early June and had barely won a victory. Eager to redeem his reputation, he requested permission to make one of his famous raids behind enemy lines. Lee reluctantly agreed, on the condition that Stuart remain in contact with the army and keep Lee informed of Hooker's movements. Stuart rode off but soon became trapped behind the advancing Union army. As a result, Lee marched into Pennsylvania virtually blind.

General Robert E. Lee.
Commanding the Confederate Army of Northern Virginia, Lee invaded Pennsylvania in the summer of 1863 to take the war out of Virginia and defeat the enemy on its own ground. Lee, however, did not want to risk a battle until his entire army was concentrated in Pennsylvania. He did not plan to engage the Federals at Gettysburg, but when battle was joined, he refused to back down.

Hooker cautiously pursued Lee on a near parallel course to the east with about 93,000 men. During this crucial time, Hooker resigned his position in a dispute with General in Chief Henry Halleck over the use of the garrison at Harpers Ferry, West Virginia, and was replaced on June 28 by Major General George Gordon Meade.

While gathering supplies in southern Pennsylvania, Lee learned from a spy that the Federals were closing in and began concentrating his army at Cashtown. The two armies first made contact outside Gettysburg on June 30 when a Confederate detachment went there in search of shoes. The following day the epic battle began in earnest when elements of Lieutenant General A. P. Hill's Confederate III Corps clashed with Brigadier General John Buford's Union cavalry division west of town. Buford held his ground until the mid-morning arrival of Major General John F. Reynolds and his I Corps. Neither Lee nor Meade wanted a major battle until all of their forces were concentrated, but the fight at Gettysburg quickly took on a life of its own. Heavy fighting continued, especially around a railroad cut, and Reynolds was killed by a Confederate sharpshooter. Reynolds's corps was forced back to Seminary Ridge and at about noon Major General Oliver O. Howard's XI Corps arrived to reinforce it. Howard turned his corps over to Major General Carl Schurz, assumed command of the field, and extended the Union right wing north of town.

By chance, Lieutenant General Richard S. Ewell's Confederate II Corps arrived on the field along the Harrisburg Road as the battle was becoming a stalemate. Positioned northeast of the XI Corps, Ewell was in an excellent position to crush the Union flank. He quickly put in Major General Robert Rodes's division on Hill's left to help stabilize the line, and Rodes engaged in fierce fighting. Ewell then sent Major General Jubal A. Early's division against the Union right flank, held by Brigadier General Francis C. Barlow's division. Barlow was wounded and captured, and his division was pushed back. A general Confederate advance then sent the Federals fleeing back through Gettysburg with the loss of thousands of prisoners. Union Major General Winfield Scott Hancock, who had arrived to take command, rallied the men on Cemetery Hill south of town and prepared to make a stand there. Lee ordered Ewell to take this high ground if possible, but Ewell failed to do so for a variety of reasons.

Meade arrived at Cemetery Hill that night and after meeting with his generals decided to hold the high ground and fight. By the morning of July 2, the Union line resembled an inverted fishhook. Culp's Hill anchored the extreme right flank and served as the hook's barb. The "shank" ran west to Cemetery Hill and then curved south along Cemetery Ridge, ending at the extreme left flank, or "eye," at Little Round Top and Big Round Top. The Confederates paralleled Meade's line, occupying Gettysburg to the north and Seminary Ridge to the west.

Lee wanted to renew the attack on the morning of July 2, but it took time to work out the assault's details. A plan

A view of Gettysburg from the west, where the battle began. Cemetery Hill is at the extreme top right corner.

finally was developed to launch a massive attack with Lieutenant General James Longstreet's I Corps against Meade's left flank, while Ewell demonstrated against the right flank, turning it into a formal attack if possible. Longstreet disapproved of the plan, preferring to place the army in a defensive position in Meade's rear, forcing him to attack. Longstreet's misgivings about Lee's tactics later led some to accuse him of being slow to carry out his orders. The assault finally was made at about 4:00 P.M., and very heavy fighting occurred in the "Wheatfield," "Devil's Den," and on Little Round Top. To the north, Ewell bombarded Cemetery and Culp's Hills and then attacked very late in the day. More vicious fighting occurred on the wooded slopes of Culp's Hill, and Early's division made a dramatic twilight assault on two Union batteries atop Cemetery Hill. Meade, however, skillfully used his interior line to shift units to threatened positions and held his ground. Early briefly captured Cemetery Hill, but a lack of support and a determined Union counterattack finally threw him back.

Against Longstreet's advice, Lee attacked again on July 3. Believing Meade must have weakened his center on July 2 to reinforce the flanks, he decided to make his main attack there. Longstreet was ordered to assemble a strike force around Major General George Pickett's fresh division. Lee also ordered Stuart, who finally arrived on the field on July 2, to raid behind the Union position and for Ewell to continue his assault on Culp's Hill. Meade correctly guessed Lee's intentions and warned Hancock to be ready in the center. Bloody fighting erupted at daylight on Culp's Hill when the Federals tried to dislodge the Confederates who had gained a foothold there. Then at 1:00 P.M., Longstreet opened a heavy artillery bombardment on Cemetery Ridge and sent 13,000 men forward at about 3:00 P.M. Pickett's Charge covered a mile of open ground, and the Confederates were raked by artillery and musketry fire the entire way. A few hundred soldiers managed to reach the Union line but were killed or captured in a fierce, but short, hand-to-hand melee. Pickett lost over half of his men, and four Confederate generals were casualties. Hancock also was seriously wounded but survived to fight another day. On other parts of the battlefield, Stuart was repulsed when he engaged David M. Gregg's Union cavalry, and on the far Union left, Major General H. Judson Kilpatrick ordered a foolish suicidal cavalry attack that led to the deaths of Brigadier General Elon J. Farnsworth and many of his men.

Lee remained in place on July 4 hoping Meade would attack him. When Meade refused, Lee began his retreat back to Virginia that night. The three-day battle was the largest of the war, and the largest ever fought in the Western Hemisphere, with Lee losing perhaps 28,000 men, while Meade counted approximately 23,000 casualties. Sometimes referred to as the "High Water Mark of the Confederacy," Gettysburg marked the peak of Confederate power. Since Lee's retreat occurred the same day Union Major General Ulysses S. Grant captured Vicksburg, Mississippi, the battle also is seen as a major turning point in the war.

Gettysburg has proven to be the most popular battle of the war—more literature has been written on it than on any other single event in American history. Much of this interest centers around the bitter fighting on Cemetery Ridge, Little Round Top, and Pickett's Charge. One of the most important landmarks of that great field, however, is Cemetery Hill, the critical high ground that anchored the Union line and that part of the Union line that lay closest to town. Cemetery Hill was the scene of some of the battle's most desperate combat and dramatic moments. It was where the Union survivors rallied at the end of the first day's battle, was subjected to a fierce Confederate artillery bombardment on the second day, and was the target of a determined twilight assault that came close to breaking the Union line.

CHAPTER 1

THE CONFEDERATES

THROUGHOUT THE MORNING of July 1, 1863, Lieutenant General Richard S. Ewell's Confederate II Corps was rapidly marching toward Gettysburg from the northeast down the Harrisburg Road. Ewell, a forty-six-year-old Virginian, became friends with future Union generals George H. Thomas and William T. Sherman before graduating from West Point in 1840. He served on the frontier in both the Sante Fe and Oregon Trail expeditions and was brevetted for gallantry in the Mexican War while serving with the dragoons as part of General Winfield Scott's escort. After the war, Ewell fought Apaches in Arizona and became one of the army's outstanding frontier officers. To honor his successful negotiations for the release of a white Apache captive, Arizona even made him an honorary delegate to its constitutional convention and named one its first four counties after him. Ewell County later was abolished because of Ewell's Confederate service, however, and became Pima and Santa Cruz counties. Other Arizona landmarks named for Ewell include Ewell Pass (modern-day Apache Pass), Ewell's Spring, and Old Baldy Peak.

Resigning his captain's commission when Virginia seceded in 1861, Ewell entered Confederate service as a lieutenant colonel of cavalry and swiftly rose through the ranks to become a brigade and division commander. He was slightly wounded in the shoulder in an 1861 skirmish, had several

**Lieutenant General Richard S. Ewell.
Although eccentric and sometimes
profane, the one-legged Ewell was a
fighter and was chosen by Lee to
replace the fallen Stonewall Jackson
in command of the II Corps. The
Gettysburg Campaign was his first
action as a corps commander. Ewell
began the campaign with great
promise, but his actions at
Gettysburg created a controversy
that persists to today.**

horses shot from under him, and lost his left leg to amputation when a bullet shattered his knee and lower leg at the
Battle of Groveton in August 1862. Ewell had been a splen-
did fighter and survivor, and was the obvious choice to
replace Thomas J. "Stonewall" Jackson after Jackson was
mortally wounded at Chancellorsville. At five feet, eight
inches in height and 140 pounds, Ewell had a sun-wrinkled
face, large bald head, and piercing gray eyes. When people
commented on his bald head and bushy beard, he wryly
noted that it was because he used his head more than his
mouth. Ewell also spoke with a slight lisp, which made his
frequent outbursts of profanity somewhat amusing. After
marrying his first cousin, the widowed Lizinka Campbell
Brown, in 1863, Ewell surprised onlookers by often intro-
ducing her as "my wife, Mrs. Brown."

Ewell's corps was one of the finest in the Army of
Northern Virginia, with three divisions of tested veterans
under the command of Major Generals Edward Johnson,
Robert Rodes, and Jubal A. Early. Early was destined to play
a major role in the fighting for Cemetery Hill. A forty-six-
year-old Virginian, he graduated from West Point in 1837

but had little military experience prior to the Civil War. After leaving the academy, Early served for about a year with the artillery but then resigned his commission to become a lawyer. He served one term in the Virginia legislature and then volunteered for service in the Mexican War but saw no combat. In 1861, Early was a delegate to the Virginia secession convention, where he voted against secession. Like many other reluctant rebels, however, he offered his services to his native state when war erupted and was commissioned colonel of the 24th Virginia Infantry.

Early earned a reputation for being a capable, hard fighting officer. Nearly six feet tall and weighing 170 pounds, he was larger than the average man, but arthritis caused a noticeable stoop in his posture, and he seemed smaller and older than he really was. Early also was known to have an irascible personality, perhaps brought on by pain from his arthritic joints. One staff officer recalled he had a "snarling, raspy disposition," while another remembered "his wit was quick, his satire biting, lurid and picturesque." Early was popular with his men, who referred to him as "Old Jube" or "Old Jubilee," but Robert E. Lee referred to him as simply "my bad old man."

Major General Jubal A. Early. Lee's "bad old man," Early commanded the Confederate division that helped crush the Federals on Gettysburg's first day of battle, and he was put in command of the twilight attack on Cemetery Hill on the second day. Early was an excellent division commander, but some of his tactical decisions at Gettysburg raised questions among his comrades.

Early was promoted to brigadier general for his good service at First Manassas. During the 1862 Peninsula Campaign, he was severely wounded at Williamsburg but recovered in time to fight at Second Manassas, Antietam, and Fredericksburg. Early's ability won him promotion to major general and command of Ewell's division when Ewell took over the II Corps. In the summer of 1863, he was one of the army's finest commanders.

Early's division included the brigades of Harry T. Hays, John B. Gordon, William "Extra Billy" Smith, and Robert Hoke. Two of these brigades would see heavy fighting on Cemetery Hill. Hays's 1,200-man brigade was the famous 1st Louisiana Brigade, consisting of the 5th, 6th, 7th, 8th, and 9th Louisiana Volunteers. In nearly all of the army's campaigns, these soldiers had earned a reputation for being outstanding shock troops. During Jackson's 1862 Shenandoah Valley Campaign, the Louisiana Brigade played the key role in winning the battles of Front Royal, First Winchester, and Port Republic. It performed admirably during the Second Manassas Campaign and fought valiantly in Antietam's infamous cornfield, losing sixty percent of its men in only thirty minutes of combat. At Salem Church it broke through two Union lines before being stopped by a third, and on the march to Gettysburg, it was the Louisiana Brigade—for the second time in the war—that stormed the heights of Winchester and wrestled it from enemy hands. Two weeks prior to Gettysburg, Ewell told one officer that next to God, he was most indebted to the Louisiana Brigade for the victory at Second Winchester.

But it was not only fighting Yankees that made the Louisiana Brigade famous. The men were also known to be among the most unruly soldiers in the entire army. Many of them were foreigners from Ireland and the Germanic states; hundreds more were French Creoles. Some were mercenary veterans of foreign wars, and it was rumored that several regiments had recruited men out of the New Orleans jails. If all of this were not enough, many of the men could speak little or no English. They brought with them to the army a lifetime of experience in fighting, stealing, and drinking. Upon reaching Virginia in 1861, the Louisianians wreaked havoc as they brawled, rioted, and drank. Some of the rowdier men were members of one company called the Tiger Rifles, and two members of this unit became the first soldiers to be executed in the Army of Northern Virginia after they attacked one of their officers. This company created so much mayhem that soon all Louisianians in Virginia were dubbed the "Louisiana Tigers."

At Gettysburg, the commander of the Tigers was Brigadier General Harry Thompson Hays, a Mississippian by birth, who began a law practice in New Orleans. He was a veteran of the Mexican War, an active member of the Whig Party, and the brother of famed Texas Indian fighter Jack Hays. In 1861, Harry Hays was elected colonel of the 7th Louisiana and proved to be a hard drinking, hard fighting officer who quickly earned his men's respect. He also had a sense of humor, and it was upon his suggestion that the army began using the tune "Yankee Doodle" to drum disgraced soldiers out of service rather than the traditional "Rogue's March,"

Brigadier General Harry T. Hays. Commanding the brigade of Louisiana Tigers in Early's division, Hays often had his hands full trying to control his men's rowdy behavior. The brigade, however, was among Lee's best and was chosen to spearhead the assault on Cemetery Hill. The Tigers' reputation as premier shock troops would be enhanced at Gettysburg.

because, as Hays claimed, more rogues marched to the tune of "Yankee Doodle" on any given day than to any other song.

Hays had extensive combat experience. His regiment had been part of Jubal Early's brigade at First Manassas and there helped crush the Union flank late in the day. Under Brigadier General Richard Taylor, Hays swept through the Shenandoah Valley with Stonewall Jackson and received a serious wound at Port Republic. When Taylor was promoted and transferred west, he recommended Hays's promotion to brigadier general and command of the 1st Louisiana Brigade. Hays soon had his hands full trying to tame the Tigers. Around Fredericksburg during the winter of 1862–1863, the brigade lived up to its reputation for thievery and mischief. So many civilians complained of the Tigers' depredations that Early constantly ordered Hays to improve discipline. After weeks of such pressure, Hays finally rebelled and tried to get his brigade transferred out of Early's division. Early called all of the brigade's colonels into his tent one day and berated them for the thievery and attempt to leave his command. He told them "no one in this army would have such a damn pack of thieves but me. If you can find any major general in this army that is damn fool enough to take you, then you may go." The brigade remained; perhaps Early was right and no one really wanted the Tigers. During the Chancellorsville Campaign, however, Hays made amends at the Battle of Salem Church outside Fredericksburg on May 3, 1863. Early and Lee watched as the Tigers smashed through two Union lines and appeared to be rolling the Yankees back into the Rappahannock River. In his excitement, Early threw his hat to the ground and cried out, "Those damned Louisiana fellows may steal as much as they please now!"

Besides Hays's brigade, the other brigade in Early's division to play a major role at Cemetery Hill was that of Robert Hoke. Hoke, however, had been wounded at Chancellorsville and Colonel Isaac E. Avery was in command at Gettysburg. Avery's brigade contained about 900 men and included the 6th, 21st, and 57th North Carolina Regiments.

Avery was thirty-five years old and a member of a prominent Tarheel family. He had attended the University of North Carolina for a year but then dropped out of school to manage his family's farm. In 1861, Avery was working for a railroad, but he resigned his position to raise a company for the 6th North Carolina and entered Confederate service as its captain. Wounded at First Manassas, he was promoted to lieutenant colonel in June 1862 and then to colonel ten days later when Dorsey Pender was promoted to brigadier general. Avery led the regiment during the Seven Days Campaign but again was badly wounded at Malvern Hill. A year later, when brigade commander Robert Hoke was wounded at Chancellorsville, Avery was given temporary command of the North Carolina brigade for the Gettysburg Campaign. A large man at over two hundred pounds, Avery was cheerful, outgoing, and well liked. He also was a scrapper in combat. As one of his men declared, "there was no fall back in Capt. Avery."

CHAPTER 2

THE FEDERALS

AMONG THOSE FEDERALS MARCHING toward Gettysburg on July 1, 1863, was Major General Oliver Otis Howard and his ill-fated XI Corps. An intensely religious, thirty-two-year-old Maine native, Howard graduated from Bowdoin College in 1850 when he was nineteen and then entered West Point. Before graduating in 1854, he became close friends with future Confederate Major General J. E. B. Stuart. After service in the Ordnance Department, Howard returned to the academy in 1857 to teach mathematics.

Married with three children, Howard considered becoming an Episcopal priest. Although he ultimately decided to remain in the military, religion became a consuming passion, and he refused alcohol, taught Bible classes at the academy, and studied theology. During the Civil War, an artillery officer wrote of Howard, "He is the only religious man of high rank that I know of in the army and, in the little intercourse I have had with him, shewed himself the most polished gentleman I have met." Because of his deep religious convictions, Howard was personally offended when the First Battle of Manassas was fought on a Sunday. He also admitted to a great initial fear during the battle, but claimed that a prayer restored his composure.

When the Civil War began, Howard was a lieutenant at West Point, but he resigned that commission in 1861 to accept an appointment as colonel of the 3rd Maine. One of

Major General Oliver Otis Howard. The ill-fated Howard was an intensely religious officer who did not drink and detested cursing. He lost his right arm earlier in the war and saw his XI Corps smashed by Confederate Lieutenant General Thomas "Stonewall" Jackson two months earlier at Chancellorsville. Described as "brave enough and a most perfect gentleman," Howard would see history repeat itself at Gettysburg.

his men described him as a "pale young man . . . slender with earnest eyes, a profusion of flowing moustache and beard." At five feet, nine inches in height (one inch taller that Ewell), Howard had blue eyes and was said by another soldier to be a "very pleasant, affable, well dressed little gentleman." One lowly orderly was impressed when Howard thanked him for holding his horse's reigns while he mounted. "Nobody said that to me before since I have been in the service," the orderly remembered.

Howard was given a brigade command, but it was routed from the field at First Manassas. Promoted to brigadier general nonetheless, he fought with the Army of the Potomac in the Peninsula Campaign and lost his right arm to amputation after suffering two wounds at Seven Pines. For his gallantry in the battle, Howard was awarded the Medal of Honor in 1893. After recovering from his wounds, he rejoined the army during the Antietam Campaign and temporarily assumed command of the division when his superior, John Sedgwick, was wounded. Promoted to major general in November 1862, Howard next led a division at Fredericksburg. When Joseph Hooker took command of the Army of the Potomac in early 1863, he appointed his friend Daniel Sickles commander of the III Corps. This presented something of a predicament because, while Sickles's and Howard's brigadier general commissions were dated the same day, Howard had been a more senior colonel. Thus, Howard had a strong claim that he should have been given the corps command. To smooth things over, Hooker placed Howard in command of the German-dominated XI Corps in March 1863.

Howard soon found his new position was not without problems. His Germans resented him for replacing the popular Franz Sigel, and they found Howard's teetotaler nature, unhumorous manner, and strict religious code unsettling. Howard disliked cursing and once pulled aside a wagon master and quietly admonished him for using profanity. He also discovered that his second-in-command, Major General Carl Schurz, was jealous and sometimes conspired against him. In a prophetic statement, Colonel Charles S. Wainwright, commander of the I Corps artillery, wrote, "Howard . . . is brave enough and a most perfect gentleman. He is a Christian as well as a man of ability, but there is some doubt as to his having snap enough to manage the Germans who require to be ruled with a rod of iron."

Many Union soldiers disliked Howard's "Dutch" corps because of its foreign makeup. Their dislike intensified after the corps' lackluster performance at Chancellorsville in May 1863. There, Howard failed to follow Hooker's orders to secure his flank and thus was crushed when Stonewall Jackson attacked late on the afternoon of May 2. Although the incident tarnished Howard's reputation, he remained in command of the XI Corps and was eager to redeem his unit's honor.

Howard's corps contained three divisions. The 1st Division would play the most critical role at Cemetery Hill. It was under Brigadier General Francis Channing Barlow, a twenty-nine-year-old Harvard graduate. Quitting his New York law practice when the war began, he joined a ninety-day

**Union Brigadier General
Francis C. Barlow.**

regiment as a private but after his enlistment expired was appointed lieutenant colonel of the 61st New York. Promoted to colonel in April 1862, Barlow led the regiment in the Peninsula Campaign. He later was severely wounded at Antietam but won a promotion to brigadier general and was given command of an XI Corps brigade. After fighting at Chancellorsville, Barlow assumed command of the division.

Barlow's two brigades were destined to see heavy fighting at Cemetery Hill. Colonel Leopold von Gilsa, a profane former Prussian officer who barely spoke English, commanded the 1st Brigade, which included the 41st, 54th, and 68th New York, and the 153rd Pennsylvania. This brigade was made up largely of German immigrants—in fact, two-thirds of the officers in the 41st New York were veterans of European wars. Union Major General Carl Schurz described von Gilsa as "one of the bravest of men and an uncommonly skillful officer." He had been wounded at Cross Keys, and at Chancellorsville he had the misfortune of commanding the corps' right flank, which was smashed by Stonewall Jackson. During the Chancellorsville disaster, when the Army of the Potomac seemed to be disintegrating, Howard met von Gilsa and told him to put his trust in

God. The colonel shocked the pious Howard by letting loose such a stream of obscenities that Howard thought him insane. On the march to Gettysburg, the colonel also ran afoul of Barlow when he disobeyed strict orders to keep the men in line and allowed more than one man at a time to leave the ranks to get water. For this minor infraction, Barlow placed von Gilsa under arrest.

Barlow's 2nd Brigade was led by Brigadier General Adelbert Ames, a twenty-eight-year-old Maine native who went to sea before entering West Point. Graduating in 1861, he became a lieutenant in the 5th U.S. Artillery and was seriously wounded in the thigh at First Manassas but continued to sit on the cannon's caisson and direct his guns until he became too weak to continue. For this bravery, Ames was awarded the Medal of Honor in 1893. After recuperating from his wound, Ames returned to the army and led a battery in the 5th U.S. Artillery during the Peninsula Campaign. He then was appointed colonel of the 20th

Brigadier General Adelbert Ames. Only two years out of West Point, Ames led a brigade while marching to Gettysburg. Cool and clear headed, he was "the best kind of a man to be associated with" and took over the division early in the battle. When the Confederates attacked Cemetery Hill, it was Ames's old brigade that bore the brunt of the assault.

Maine in August 1862 and led it at Fredericksburg. Ames's service there won him another promotion to brigadier general, even though he had never commanded any unit larger than a regiment. Only two years out of West Point, he was known to be kind, cool, and clear headed. Colonel Wainwright was particularly impressed with Ames because he did not hear the young brigadier swear one oath during the entire three-day battle at Gettysburg, "a strange thing in this army," he noted. Wainwright also wrote that Ames was "the best kind of a man to be associated with, cool and clear in his own judgment, gentlemanly and without the smallest desire to interfere." Ames's brigade included the 17th Connecticut and the 25th, 75th, and 107th Ohio.

Colonel Andrew L. Harris commanded Ames's 75th Ohio. A twenty-eight-year-old Ohio native, he was raised on a farm but graduated from Miami University in 1860. When war began, Harris gave up the study of law to enter Union service as a lieutenant in the ninety-day 20th Ohio. When the unit disbanded, he raised a company for the 75th Ohio in October 1861 and became its captain. A battle-tested veteran, Harris had been severely wounded in the arm at the Battle of McDowell and fought at Cedar Mountain and Second Manassas. He was promoted to major in January

Colonel Andrew L. Harris. A twenty-eight-year-old Ohio native, Harris had been wounded at the Battle of McDowell while serving as a company captain in the 75th Ohio. When his colonel was killed at Chancellorsville in May 1863, Harris was promoted to command the regiment. Gettysburg was his initiation as a regimental commander, and before the fight was over he found himself leading the brigade defending Cemetery Hill.

1863, and when his colonel was killed at Chancellorsville, he was made colonel. Gettysburg was Harris's first engagement as a regimental colonel and before the fight was over, he would be commanding the brigade.

Howard's 2nd and 3rd Divisions, under Brigadier General Baron Adolph Wilhelm August Friedrich von Steinwehr and Major General Carl Schurz, respectively, played supporting roles at Cemetery Hill. The forty-year-old von Steinwehr was a native of the Duchy of Brunswick and was the son and grandson of army officers, his grandfather having been a Prussian general who fought Napoleon. After attending a local military academy, he served as a lieutenant in the duchy's army but took a leave of absence in 1847 to come to the United States to try to secure a commission to fight in the Mexican War. He failed in his quest but was hired by the Unites States' topographical engineers and helped survey the border with Mexico. Afterward, von Steinwehr was sent to conduct survey work in Alabama, where he married an Alabama woman before returning to Europe in 1849. He immigrated back to the United States in 1854 and settled in Connecticut to farm.

Von Steinwehr entered Union service in 1861 as colonel of the German-dominated 29th New York and was held in reserve during the First Battle of Manassas. Promoted to brigadier general in October, he was given a brigade command in Louis Blenker's division and fought in the 1862 Shenandoah Valley Campaign before being given a division command in June 1862. The division saw heavy combat at Second Manassas, but missed Antietam, and then was assigned to Howard's XI Corps. At Chancellorsville, von Steinwehr was one of the corps' few officers who took precautions against a flank attack by erecting earthworks, but his division was still overrun and routed by Stonewall Jackson. Howard praised von Steinwehr for being "cool, collected and judicious" during the battle, and he continued to be well respected by both officers and men. Brigadier General Alpheus Williams described him as being a

Brigadier General Baron Adolph Wilhelm August Friedrich von Steinwehr. A military-trained native of the Duchy of Brunswick, von Steinwehr immigrated to the U.S. before the war. Put in command of a German-dominated XI Corps division, he was described as "cool, collected and judicious." Although he was among those routed two months earlier at Chancellorsville, von Steinwehr was an "officer of great merit" and helped defend Cemetery Hill.

"remarkably intelligent and agreeable person," and one of his soldiers recalled the general was "an officer of great merit, trained in the German school and possessing the confidence of his superiors." Because of this respect, von Steinwehr retained his division command and led his two brigades, under Colonels Charles R. Coster and Orland Smith, to Gettysburg.

Although Schurz's 3rd Division only played a supporting role at Cemetery Hill, he became a key figure in the battle because he temporarily led the corps. Schurz was a thirty-three-year-old Prussian native. After attending school at Cologne, he received a doctorate at the University of Bonn, where he became an exceptional speaker associated with the revolutionary movement sweeping Europe. Schurz participated in the failed 1848 revolutions but managed to escape capture by fleeing to Switzerland. In 1850, he secretly slipped back into Prussia, rescued a prominent revolutionary from Spandau Prison, and fled with him to England. Schurz taught in England and France, but the latter country finally expelled him, and he and his wife eventually moved to the United States in 1852. Settling in Pennsylvania, he became a popular public speaker and abolitionist. Schurz later moved to Wisconsin, where he became active in the Republican Party and helped win Abraham Lincoln the German vote in the 1860 presidential election. Lincoln appointed him minister to Spain in 1861, but Schurz returned to the United States in 1862 and pressured Lincoln for a commission and the immediate emancipation of the slaves. Although Lincoln refused the latter, he did appoint Schurz a brigadier general to gain support from German Americans.

Schurz was an impressive figure. Tall and polished, with curly brown hair and a reddish beard, he was charming and gave "the impression of being a man of ability." After leading a I Corps division at Second Manassas, Schurz was given command of the XI Corps' 3rd Division. Promoted to major general in March 1863, he was among those routed by Stonewall Jackson at Chancellorsville. By the time of the Gettysburg Campaign, Howard had become uneasy about his subordinate. Schurz seemed to be scheming with other officers to get the corps returned to the command of fellow German Franz Sigel, and Schurz's connections to Lincoln were well known. At Gettysburg, Schurz's division included

Major General Carl Schurz. A Prussian revolutionary, Schurz immigrated to the U.S. before the war and became an abolitionist and active Republican. Appointed general by Abraham Lincoln, he was one of many Civil War political generals and would play a supportive role at Cemetery Hill with his division.

the brigades of Brigadier General Alexander Schimmelfennig and Colonel Wladimir Krzyzanowski.

On the Taneytown Road, far behind the XI Corps on the morning of July 1, was thirty-nine-year-old Major General Winfield Scott Hancock and his II Corps. One of twin brothers, Hancock was a native of Pennsylvania, an 1844 West Point graduate, and a veteran of the Mexican War. Early in the Civil War, he was appointed a brigadier general of volunteers and was given command of a brigade in the Army of the Potomac's II Corps. Hancock's outstanding performance in the 1862 Peninsula Campaign earned him the *nom de guerre* "Hancock the Superb." He took command of the division when his superior was killed at Antietam, fought well at Fredericksburg and Chancellorsville, and assumed command of the corps after the latter battle.

Although new to corps command, the dashing and handsome Hancock was one of the army's rising stars, and General Meade would rely heavily on him in defending Gettysburg's high ground.

CHAPTER 3

JULY 1, 1863

ON THE MORNING OF JULY L, 1863, the Battle of Gettysburg began west of town when A. P. Hill's Confederate I Corps attacked Brigadier General John Buford's Union cavalrymen. Buford contested the enemy advance alone until the mid-morning arrival of Major General John F. Reynolds's I Corps. Assuming command of the field, Reynolds deployed his units and was savagely attacked by Hill's Confederates. Soon, Reynolds fell victim to an enemy sharpshooter, and his men struggled to hold the line. During the fighting, Howard arrived in advance of the XI Corps to inspect the ground and stopped on Cemetery Hill, just south of town. He and his adjutant general, Lieutenant Colonel Theodore Meysenburg, quickly realized the significance of the position. On the hill was located the Evergreen Cemetery and a large, arched, two-story brick gatehouse. From atop the hill, artillery could command the town itself and the hills and wood lots to the north and west. After taking in the panoramic view, Howard remarked, "This seems to be a good position, colonel," to which Meysenburg replied, "It is the only position, general."

Mounting their horses, the officers galloped down Cemetery Hill into town. Soldiers there took Howard to the roof of a nearby building to get a better look at the battle raging outside Gettysburg. He was still observing the area when a cavalry sergeant rode up and shouted from below

Union Brigadier General John Buford.

Confederate Lieutenant General A. P. Hill.

Union Major General John F. Reynolds.

that Reynolds had been wounded. Within minutes it was learned that Reynolds, in fact, was dead. Thrust into command of the field, Howard immediately sent a flurry of orders. He informed Schurz what had happened and told him to assume command of the XI Corps and hurry to Gettysburg. Howard also sent word for Major General Daniel Sickles's III Corps and Major General Henry Slocum's XII Corps to hurry along. He then established his headquarters on top of Cemetery Hill just across the Baltimore Pike from the cemetery gatehouse.

As Howard took command of the battlefield, his XI Corps rushed toward Gettysburg along the Emmitsburg and Taneytown Roads. Justus Silliman, a member of the 17th Connecticut in Ames's brigade, wrote, "the roads were muddy and the march very tiresome as we were pushed forward in great haste. On arriving to within about three miles of the town we heard the cannonading and for the first time it entered our minds that we might soon have some fighting to do." At about 12:30 P.M., the corps arrived at Gettysburg, with Schurz's division, temporarily commanded by Schimmelfennig, in the lead and Barlow close behind. Marching down Washington Street, the men were met by enthusiastic citizens who cheered and offered food and drink. Silliman recalled, "The citizens lined the streets holding cups of water for the thirsty, but we had no time to stop but passed through almost on the double quick and took our position on the right of the town." As they approached the battlefield, Barlow had released von Gilsa from arrest and placed him back at the head of his brigade. A Gettysburg resident remembered the dramatic scene as the brigade passed through town:

> Far down the road, behind the passing regiments, a
> roar of cheers began. It rolled forward, faster than the
> running of the men who made it—like some high
> surge sweeping across the surface of a flowing sea.
> Its roar of cheering neared and neared, until we saw

Postwar photograph of the intersection of the Baltimore Pike (left) and the Emmitsburg Road (right). Cemetery Hill is a few hundred yards down the Baltimore Pike to the left of the photo.

Looking down Baltimore Street from the base of Cemetery Hill.

a group of officers coming at a brisk trot, with the mighty cheer always at their horses' heels. Among them rode one man in colonel's uniform who held his head high and smiled. . . . [von Gilsa] was on his way into action, and the whole brigade that knew him was greeting him with the chorus of the lungs.

Howard quickly ordered Schurz to post the corps to the right of the I Corps to protect the flank from the Rebels approaching from the north. Schimmelfennig put his division to the right of the I Corps, and Barlow extended the line farther to the right with his division. After making other preparations, Howard returned to his headquarters on Cemetery Hill and remained there for the rest of the day.

Several miles north of Gettysburg, Ewell was hurrying his Confederate veterans toward the sound of battle, and the general seemed on edge. Having served much of his career under the rigid Stonewall Jackson, he was unused to working under the wide discretion given by Lee. Upon receiving orders on June 30 to go to Cashtown or Gettysburg, "according to circumstances," Ewell read the note several times in front of his staff. Criticizing its vague wording, he asked them what "according to circumstances" meant. "Why can't a Commanding General have someone on his staff who can write an intelligible order?" he rhetorically asked. Jedediah Hotchkiss, a cartographer, noted, "The Gen. was quite testy, hard to please, because disappointed and had every one flying around."

Rodes's division was the first unit of Ewell's corps to arrive at Gettysburg, and shortly after 2:00 P.M., it became hotly engaged with the Union I and XI Corps northwest of town. When Ewell arrived on the field, Rodes was under intense pressure from the enemy. While watching the battle develop from Oak Ridge, Ewell received orders from Lee to avoid a general engagement if the enemy was found to be in strength. Realizing it was too late to avoid a battle, however, Ewell decided to continue.

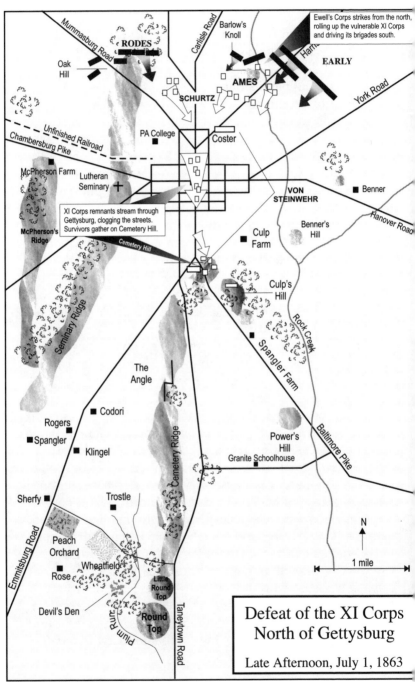

Ewell's Corps strikes from the north, rolling up the vulnerable XI Corps and driving its brigades south.

MUMMASBURG Road

RODES

Oak Hill

Carlisle Road

Barlow's Knoll

Hanover Road

EARLY

York Road

AMES

SCHURTZ

Unfinished Railroad

Chambersburg Pike

PA College

Coster

McPherson Farm

Lutheran Seminary

Benner

VON STEINWEHR

Benner's Hill

McPherson's Ridge

XI Corps remnants stream through Gettysburg, clogging the streets. Survivors gather on Cemetery Hill.

Cemetery Hill

Culp Farm

Culp's Hill

Seminary Ridge

Rock Creek

Spangler Farm

The Angle

Spangler Farm

Codori

Cemetery Ridge

Rogers

Spangler

Klingel

Power's Hill

Granite Schoolhouse

Baltimore Pike

Emmitsburg Road

Sherfy

Trostle

Peach Orchard

Wheatfield

Rose

Devil's Den

Little Round Top

Round Top

Plum Run

Taneytown Road

N

1 mile

Defeat of the XI Corps
North of Gettysburg

Late Afternoon, July 1, 1863

Theodore P. Savas

When Early approached the field along the Harrisburg Road, he was perfectly positioned to attack Barlow's division on the extreme right flank of the XI Corps. Early placed Gordon's brigade on the right of the road, Hays's brigade astride and to the left of the road, and Avery's brigade on Hays's left. At approximately 3:45 P.M., Gordon attacked. Captain William J. Seymour, Hays's assistant adjutant general, wrote, "The musketry was very severe and we feared that Gordon would be borne back; but in a few minutes the firing ceased, & the smoke lifting from the field, revealed to our sight the defeated Federals in disorderly flight, hotly pursued by the gallant Georgians." Early then sent in Hays and Avery, who advanced down the road toward the Almshouse. In the vicious attack, Barlow was severely wounded. Left on the field, he was captured after his men retreated. Ames then turned his brigade over to Colonel Andrew L. Harris and assumed command of the division. Seeing the Federals reeling, Lee ordered a general assault along the entire line, and the Union line collapsed.

The 17th Connecticut was among Ames's regiments that were hit hard, and its Lieutenant Colonel Douglas Fowler was killed. Private William H. Warren remembered that Fowler was riding a conspicuous white horse and was urging his men in a futile counterattack when he was struck. Warren wrote, "Lieut. Col. Fowler was killed, his head shot off and his brains flew on the Adjutant [H. Whitney Chatfield]." Two soldiers tried to put Fowler on a horse, but their strength failed them and they had to abandon the body. Aware of their dire predicament, Private Warren and others ran south toward the Almshouse. Warren wrote,

> Rufus Warren fell, he was about a rod ahead of me, he fell the opposite way he was running then throwed up his hands and hollowed *O Dear, Help me, Help me*, it was not time for me to stop so I kept on before I had hard[ly] gone a rod fother a bullet cut a hole out of my pants ... but did not touch

me ... bullets were comeing in a shower I thought
I was spoke for, still kept moveing on and shortly I
expect it was a piece of spent shell struck my right
shoulder blade and almost knocked me over. ...

Hays's Tigers next smashed Harris's brigade around the
Almshouse and sent the Union line in retreat once more.
Ewell's Confederates then encountered Colonel Charles R.
Coster's brigade from von Steinwehr's XI Corps division at
John Kuhn's brickyard. It, too, was crushed, and scores of
men surrendered. From atop Cemetery Hill, Howard wit-
nessed the disaster and sent orders for Schurz to withdraw
to the high ground.

Lieutenant J. Warren Jackson, of the 8th Louisiana, was in
the midst of the Confederate assault and wrote his brother
afterward:

[A]rrived at Gettysburg at 3 P.M. Formed line of battle and loaded. Could see Rodes on our right driving the Yankees before him like sheep. It was the
prettiest sight I ever saw. At 5 minutes past 3 we
started forward & marched slowly in line for 1½
miles before we got to any yankees. We crossed
about 20 fences & 1 creek and at last came right slap
up on the "11th corps" & a battery. We ran them thro
town & caught more prisoners than we had men in
the brigade. We also captured 2 pieces out of the battery. We ran them thro town & caught hundreds of
them in the houses & cellars. ... We formed line of
battle in town & Co. I. had to go out as skirmishers—the enemy were posted on Cemetery Hill
about 600 yards from town & had command of
every place near town or around it—our position
was a poor one and as we deployed we were subjected to a galling fire from their sharpshooters.
Nobody hurt and we soon laid low in the grass but
their position was such a good one that they could

see us and they kept up their firing and I spent about 2 hours as miserably as I ever did in my life. . . .

Captain Seymour was one of many Tigers who helped gather up the hundreds of prisoners. After the war, he wrote of the Union collapse,

On we pushed, driving the enemy in great confusion upon the town, taking whole regiments belonging to the 11th Corps. One Dutch Colonel at the head of about 250 men came up to me and cried out that he surrendered. . . . I made him throw his sword upon the ground and sent the whole party back to our rear guard under the escort of only one Confederate soldier.

Besides two cannons, Seymour estimated Hays's brigade captured 3,000 prisoners, while Hays simply reported that he took more captives than he had men. Ewell claimed his men took about 5,000 prisoners, but the XI Corps reported only about 1,500 men missing for the entire battle.

Ewell's corps secured the town, rounded up prisoners, and took up positions in the streets to await orders. Hays's men were among the first Confederates to enter Gettysburg and moved onto East Middle Street, while Avery's brigade pushed on to confront Cemetery Hill south of town. The Tigers met some resistance in the streets from the 17th Connecticut but soon cleared the town. Seeing a bucket of water that resident William McLean had put on the curb for Union soldiers, the Tigers avoided it, thinking it might be poisoned. Later, a curious McLean looked out his window and observed some Confederates sitting on the curb rummaging through captured Union knapsacks and reading aloud the letters they found. When his five-year-old daughter began singing "Hang Jeff Davis on a Sour Apple Tree" from an open window, the horrified McLean was relieved to

Private Charles L. Comes, 8th Louisiana, one of the few Louisiana Tigers to be killed on the first day of battle at Gettysburg.

find that the Rebels paid her no attention. To the west, on the corner of Baltimore and Middle Streets, Hays's Tigers searched another house and captured approximately a dozen Union soldiers, who were escorted away. They then spread hay from a stable along the sidewalk and settled down, boasting loud enough to be heard of what they were going to do to the enemy tomorrow. The rest of the brigade advanced as far as the railroad and then moved to a position east of town.

During this time, Justus Silliman had an encounter with the Louisiana Tigers. Wounded in the head during the Confederate attack north of town, he was taken prisoner and was placed in Hays's field hospital. Silliman later wrote home:

> The rebels occasionally came in bringing sheep, chickens, etc captured at neighboring farm houses. They all seemed perfectly confident of success as they were concentrating nearly the whole of their

army of Va at this place. Occasionally some of the rebs would come up from the city with carpets, collars, shoes and other articles taken from the stores in Gettysburg. . . . The rebels with whom I conversed seemed anxious to close the war and all were anxious to see Jeff Davis and Abe Lincoln hung and many looked forward to our next presidential election in hopes that it would either bring about a reconstruction of the union or come to some terms of peace.

There were several darkees around the hospital who were waiters on Rebel officers. One of these was quite friendly and was a true union man. He said the Rebels tried to make their case as good as possible but that they were hard up.

From atop Cemetery Hill, Howard began deploying the corps' survivors at about 4:30 P.M. As the remnants of the 17th Connecticut approached (the regiment had lost 145 of its 386 men that afternoon), they were met by Howard at a stone wall near the edge of town. The general yelled out to the color sergeant, "Sergeant, plant your flag down there in that stone wall!" Not recognizing Howard, the sergeant replied, "All right, if you will go with me, I will!" Howard took up the flag and set it in the stones, and the regiment began to rally around it on the slope of the hill.

While the battle raged that July afternoon, Meade sent Major General Winfield Scott Hancock ahead of the main army to take command of the field. On the road, Hancock passed an ambulance carrying Reynolds's body to the rear. Arriving on Cemetery Hill just as Howard was preparing its defenses, Hancock saluted and tersely stated that Meade had sent him to take command. When Howard argued that he was more senior in rank, Hancock informed him that he had written orders and could show them if Howard questioned his authority. Howard declined. Meade had given Hancock orders to fall back to a more defensible ground behind Pipe Creek, but Hancock instantly recognized the high ground was a strong position and decided to stay and fight. Howard agreed, and Hancock replied, "Very well, sir, I select this as the battlefield." After the war, Howard insinuated that he and Hancock actually shared command that afternoon, but he was in error. Once Hancock arrived on Cemetery Hill, he clearly was in command of the field.

Hancock's arrival boosted Union morale, and he briefly consulted with Generals Gouverneur K. Warren and Buford before deploying the remnants of the I and XI Corps to hold the high ground at Cemetery and Culp's Hills. Wadsworth's division and the 5th Maine Artillery were sent to the western slope of Culp's Hill. Colonel Orland Smith's brigade of von Steinwehr's division was put in front of town at the base of Cemetery Hill, with Colonel Charles R. Coster's brigade and Ames's division on his right. Schurz's division was put on the left in the cemetery, artillery batteries were quickly brought up, and earthworks were erected.

Major General Winfield Scott Hancock. A West Point graduate and Mexican War veteran, Hancock already had earned the nickname "Hancock the Superb" early in the war and was put in command of the Army of the Potomac's II Corps just weeks before Gettysburg. Ordered by Meade to assume command of the field on the first day of battle, Hancock immediately saw the significance of Cemetery Hill and made the decision to hold the high ground.

While Hancock was preparing Cemetery Hill for defense, Ewell was faced with a dilemma. Lee had ordered his commanders not to bring on a general engagement because the army was not yet concentrated. But a major battle had already begun, and Ewell recognized the importance of keeping the initiative and seizing the high ground south of Gettysburg. Casualties, however, had been significant, with Rodes losing about 2,000 men. Also, two of Ewell's three divisions were disorganized and exhausted from the afternoon's fight, and his third division, under Johnson, had not yet arrived. A most important decision now faced the new corps commander. With only 7,000–8,000 men on hand, all of whom were disorganized and exhausted, should Ewell move on to attack Cemetery Hill?

Ewell had already had a narrow escape that afternoon. As he rode from Oak Ridge into Gettysburg, his horse was hit on the head by a shell fragment, and he was tossed hard to the ground. Undeterred, Ewell remounted and rode on to find Early, his most trusted subordinate. He first met Gordon, however, who urged him to press on to Cemetery Hill. At that moment, Major Henry Kyd Douglas rode up

Union Colonel Orland Smith.

Union Colonel Charles R. Coster.

and reported that Johnson's division was approaching town. Hearing the news, Gordon excitedly stated that he and Johnson could take the hill before dark. Ewell was quiet, however, and Douglas later wrote that he seemed "unusually grave and silent." Apparently contemplating Lee's orders not to bring on a general battle, Ewell finally instructed Douglas to halt Johnson when he reached town and to await orders. General Lee, he explained, was not yet on the field and had "directed me to come to Gettysburg, and I have done so. I do not feel like going further or making an attack without orders from him."

Ewell rode on into Gettysburg (probably along Carlisle Street) and received word that Lee was at Seminary Ridge. About that time, Major Walter Taylor, Lee's aide, rode up. After the war, Taylor claimed he carried Ewell Lee's orders to take the hills "if he could do so to advantage." Taylor also wrote that Ewell made no objections and left him with the impression that the order would be carried out. Taylor's claim later became an important part of the Cemetery Hill controversy, but Ewell's stepson and aide, Captain Campbell Brown, afterward claimed that Taylor never brought such orders.

Ewell next met Hays, who urged him to advance and take the hill, but the general reportedly laughed and asked if the Tigers never got enough fighting. Hays took offense at the offhand remark and snapped that he was only trying to prevent the sacrifice of his men in a later assault. After sending for Early and Rodes, Ewell then waited for them under a shade tree in the town square. When the two officers finally arrived, they informed him that some of their men had pushed through town and urged Ewell to press on, *if* Lee could provide some support on the right. Ewell agreed and sent a staff officer to inform Lee of their wishes. Riding forward on Baltimore Street to reconnoiter, Ewell and Early dodged sharpshooters' fire coming from von Steinwehr's skirmishers posted in some buildings at the base of Cemetery Hill. Turning left, they rode along an alley and High Street to put some buildings between them and the sharpshooters. During this excursion, Ewell and Early saw at least one Union brigade on top of Cemetery Hill, supported by at least forty cannons, and could not tell what lay behind the hill's crest.

By this time, Ewell had decided to attack even though Rodes's division was badly mauled, Early was missing one of his four brigades, and Johnson was not yet on the field. At that time, about 4:30 P.M., a staff officer arrived from Lee with the unsettling news that Lee had no men to support him in an attack. Lee ordered Ewell to take the hill "if practicable," but he then confused the issue by repeating his orders not to bring on a general engagement until the entire army was up. Again Ewell became upset with his commander's vague orders, for following the first would require disobeying the second. Realizing Culp's Hill, which at the time was unoccupied, was a key to the field, Ewell decided he could send Johnson to occupy it once he arrived and not violate Lee's orders against starting a general engagement.

Brigadier General Isaac Trimble, who accompanied Ewell part of the day, found Ewell's lack of aggressiveness troubling and encouraged him to move quickly. Trimble later wrote that Ewell "moved about uneasily, a good deal excited, and seemed to me to be undecided what to do next." Having personally gone over the ground and seeing the significance of Culp's Hill, Trimble urged Ewell to take it immediately. When Ewell said he would wait for Johnson, Trimble continued to push the issue, claiming he offered to take the hill himself with as little as a regiment. Ewell, tiring of the discussion, finally barked, "When I need advice from a junior officer, I generally ask it," and Trimble stormed off.

As Ewell weighed his options, another troubling report was brought to him. Although it is difficult to set the precise time, Early received word from Brigadier General William "Extra Billy" Smith, one of his brigade commanders guarding the left flank, that a Federal force was moving into Ewell's left rear along the York Turnpike. Early later claimed he did not believe this report—and it did turn out to be erroneous—but he still sent Gordon's brigade to join Smith in case the enemy was advancing along the road. Early, Ewell, and Rodes then followed the brigade to verify the report. The II Corps already was weakened from casu-

Confederate Brigadier General William "Extra Billy" Smith.

48

alties and the absence of Johnson, and now half of Early's division was down the York Turnpike, unavailable for use in any assault on the high ground.

Ewell sent two aides to scout Culp's Hill before returning to town with Early. There, he found Johnson, who reported that his men were only about a mile behind, but that a wagon train had the road blocked, and it would take them about an hour to reach town. The news greatly troubled Ewell, and he asked Early if he could take Culp's Hill immediately and have Johnson support his right wing when his division arrived. Although Early was the one who had urged quick action, he bristled at the suggestion and quipped "that his command had been doing all the hard marching and fighting and was not in condition to make the move." Johnson took offense at the remark, and he and Early began snapping at one another. As he often would do, Ewell finally deferred to Early and told him to make camp. He then ordered Johnson to bring up his men and wait for further orders.

After an exhausting twenty-five-mile march, Johnson's division finally arrived after 6:00 P.M. as the sun was setting and Ewell's scouts were returning from Culp's Hill. The scouts informed Ewell that the hill was unoccupied, but, in fact, they somehow had missed detecting the Union Iron Brigade, which was positioned on its western slope. Ewell asked Rodes what he thought of sending Johnson to take the hill. Oddly, Rodes acted disinterested and shrugged that Johnson's men were "tired and footsore" and that "he did not think it would result in anything one way or the other." Early disagreed and told Ewell, "If you do not go up there tonight, it will cost you 10,000 to get up there tomorrow." Again, Ewell agreed with Early and ordered Johnson to move to the far left and to take Culp's Hill if it was still unoccupied. Instead of advancing immediately, however, Johnson sent his own scouts up the hill to reconnoiter. Thus, as darkness closed in, Ewell mistakenly believed that Johnson had occupied the crucial hill and that he would be able to force the Federals to abandon Cemetery Hill in the morning. In reality, Culp's Hill was still in Union hands, and the Confederates had lost their narrow window of opportunity to take the high ground.

The Federals waiting on top of Cemetery Hill were unaware of the delays within the Confederate ranks and believed an attack was coming. Once their defenses were prepared that afternoon, Hancock and Schurz sat on a stone fence on the brow of Cemetery Hill and watched through binoculars as the enemy massed troops below. Schurz remembered, "I was not ashamed to own that I felt nervous, for while our position was a strong one, the infantry line in it appeared, after the losses of the day, woefully thin. It was soothing to my pride, but by no means reassuring as to our situation, when General Hancock admitted that he felt nervous, too." Still, Hancock remarked that with the artillery support then on hand, he believed they could hold out until more help arrived. As time passed, and no Confederate attack was made, the two officers began to relax. Schurz wrote afterward, "Our nerves grew more and more tranquil as minute after minute lapsed, for each brought night and reinforcements nearer." Then, at about 7:00 P.M., Major General Henry Slocum arrived with the XII Corps. Hancock turned field command over to him as the senior officer present and returned to Taneytown to inform Meade of the day's events. Later that night, Slocum posted two divisions on Culp's Hill, making it nearly impregnable.

That night, Generals Howard, Slocum, and Daniel Sickles made their headquarters on the grounds around the cemetery gatehouse. Cemetery caretaker Peter Thorn's family lived there, but Thorn at the time was in the army at Harpers Ferry, West Virginia, and the gatehouse was only occupied by his wife, Catherine Elizabeth, and her elderly father. The day had proved a trying one for Catherine. Throughout the fighting, she had cooked for soldiers and had even accompanied an officer under fire to point out the

Two views of the Evergreen Cemetery Gatehouse.

roads and other features in the area. To honor this bravery, nearby soldiers gave three cheers and a band played for her. In returning to the gatehouse, Catherine walked on the opposite side of the officer's horse to avoid enemy rifle fire coming from town. She made it home unscathed, but as soon as she climbed up to her second floor room, a Rebel shell smashed through a window and went through the ceiling. Going back downstairs, Catherine was asked by a soldier if she would prepare General Howard some supper. After returning from a fruitless mission to find some meat, she found her house filling up with wounded soldiers, including some who were lying on the kitchen floor. Gamely working around them, Catherine cooked what little she could for Howard, Slocum, and Sickles.

That night, the Army of the Potomac's cavalry corps and seven of its infantry corps were at or near Gettysburg, and two others would arrive soon. Meade rode at the head of his escort up the Taneytown Road under a bright moon and arrived at the cemetery gatehouse after midnight. Tired from his long ride, he dismounted stiffly and met with Howard, Sickles, Slocum, and a handful of other officers in the gatehouse. Over flickering candles, Howard informed Meade of Cemetery Hill's strengths, and Sickles proclaimed, "It is a good place to fight from, general!" Meade stated the obvious, "I am glad to hear you say so, gentlemen, for it is too late to leave it."

Schurz returned to the gatehouse and found in the lower room a handful of generals lounging around on the floor and on boxes, with candles providing a little light from the top of a barrel. After recounting the day's events and speculating on what the morrow would bring, they all matter-of-factly rose and bid one another good night, leaving "as that of an ordinary occasion." Schurz also left and returned to the cemetery, where he lay on the ground and fell asleep.

While the Union high command made the decision to stay and fight that night, their soldiers prepared for the bloodletting that surely would come. Private Mesnard and the 55th Ohio were positioned behind a stone wall along the Emmitsburg Road below Cemetery Hill. He wrote, "Our army was drifting in and taking position all the afternoon and night, and the artillery on both sides was thundering shells through the air." Across the way, the Confederates also spent a sleepless night. Captain Seymour remembered, "All night long the Federals were heard chopping away and working like beavers, and when day dawned the ridge was found to be crowned with strongly built fortifications and bristling with a most formidable array of cannon."

That night, Lee met with Ewell, Rodes, and Early to find out what condition the II Corps was in and what could be done the next day. Ewell seemed uncomfortable and indecisive in the presence of his superior and let Early do the talking. Lee first asked if Ewell could attack the Union right at daylight. Early spoke up, instead, and claimed that their front was steeper and rockier than the others and that the enemy had concentrated his strength there. He recommended that James Longstreet's I Corps hit the Union left, instead, and Ewell and Rodes agreed. Undoubtedly troubled by the lack of aggressiveness shown by his officers, Lee then ordered the corps to withdraw since it could not accomplish anything where it was and to move to the right to support Longstreet. Again Early interjected. He argued that it would be bad for morale to abandon the hard-won ground, the wounded men, and the captured wagons and stated that their position was well suited for defense. Again Ewell and Rodes agreed. Lee reluctantly decided to let the corps remain in position and have Longstreet make the main attack. Ewell was to make a demonstration when Longstreet advanced and to turn it into a full-scale attack if possible.

Later that night, Lee had second thoughts about Ewell's corps and sent orders for Ewell to withdraw from his position and move to the right to reinforce Longstreet. Ewell still believed a withdrawal would be bad for morale and rode to see Lee about 10:00 P.M. Ewell wanted to stay in position, largely because he believed that Johnson already had seized Culp's Hill, and from it, he could force the Federals off Cemetery Hill the next morning. Lee agreed to let Ewell remain in place, but he instructed the general not to get so entangled that he could not extricate himself, for Lee still was not sure if he wanted to fight a general battle at Gettysburg. Captain Brown claimed that this caveat "had a decided influence" on Ewell's later actions.

After midnight, Ewell returned to his headquarters, located in a barn near the intersection of Carlisle Street and Harrisburg Road, and sent an aide to tell Johnson to occupy Culp's Hill if he had not already done so. The aide soon returned with the shocking news that Johnson had not advanced as previously ordered, and the hill now was firmly in Union hands. Also an enemy courier had been captured with documents indicating that the Union XII Corps was now at Gettysburg and the V Corps would be there by dawn. Captain Brown wrote later, "I know that Gen'l Ewell held Johnson not altogether free from blame in the matter & supposed until near daylight that the hill had been taken possession of as he had directed." Ewell's actions in this matter seem strange. If, as Brown stated, he

Major General Edward Johnson. Johnson commanded a division in Ewell's Confederate corps, and Ewell hoped to use him to seize the high ground on Gettysburg's first day of battle. Johnson's late arrival, however, ruined Ewell's plan. Over the next two days, Johnson's brigades saw some of Gettysburg's bloodiest fighting on the slopes of Culp's Hill.

believed Culp's Hill had already been occupied according to his previous order, why would he have thought it necessary to send Johnson a second order late that night? Whatever the reason, the news that the crucial high ground was in enemy hands embarrassed Ewell, for he had convinced Lee to change his plans on the assumption Culp's Hill was secured. Without possession of the hill, it would have been better to have moved the II Corps to the right as Lee originally planned.

Sometime before daylight on July 2, Ewell sent Captain Brown back to Lee for clarification of his orders. Lee instructed Brown to tell Ewell to be sure not to become so much involved as to be unable readily to extricate his troops, "for I have not decided to fight here—and may probably draw off by my right flank . . . so as to get between the enemy & Washington & Baltimore & force them to attack us in position." Brown claimed, "These orders had a decided influence on Genl Ewell's movements—making him more cautious & hesitating. . . ."

CHAPTER 4

JULY 2, 1863

LEE WANTED TO ATTACK MEADE'S left wing with Longstreet's corps at daylight on July 2, but last-minute details pushed the movement back, and he had to order Ewell to delay his demonstration, as well. As the sun rose higher, Ewell impatiently sent Captain Brown to Lee to report all was ready on his front. Lee informed Brown that Longstreet was not yet in position and to tell Ewell not to begin the demonstration until he heard Longstreet's guns open fire. After awhile, Lee also became impatient with Longstreet and sent Charles Venable to ask if Ewell could attack on his front, and, if not, could he still move to the right. Ewell said no to both. An attack on the high ground without Longstreet's diversion would not succeed, and if he moved to the right in daylight, the enemy would spot him and could easily shift troops there along their interior lines. Lee was forced to keep to the original plan but postponed Longstreet's attack until later in the afternoon.

Throughout the day, the opposing armies skirmished and jockeyed for position. From the top of Cemetery Hill that morning, Schurz and his men became nervous as they watched the Confederates positioning their forces. The general recalled how

> the belts of timber screening their lines presented
> open spaces enough, in which we could see their

bayonets glisten and their artillery in position, to permit us to form a rough estimate of the extent of the positions they occupied and of the strength of their forces present.

With the Army of the Potomac not yet consolidated, Schurz could only hope that Lee would delay the coming attack.

Earlier in the day, at about 8:00 A.M., Meade rode up to Schurz's position at the cemetery, accompanied by only a staff officer and an orderly. Schurz always remembered Meade's plain appearance:

His long-bearded, haggard face, shaded by a black military felt hat the rim of which was turned down, looked careworn and tired, as if he had not slept that night. The spectacles on his nose gave him a somewhat magistorial look. There was nothing in his appearance or his bearing—not a smile nor a sympathetic word addressed to those around him—that might have made the hearts of the soldiers warm up to him, or that called forth a cheer. There was nothing of pose, nothing stagey, about him. His mind was

Major General George Gordon Meade. Formerly head of the V Corps, Meade took command of the Army of the Potomac just three days before the Battle of Gettysburg. He had a "careworn and tired" look about him when he arrived on the night of July 1, and although his men were "not enthusiastic," they were "clearly satisfied" with him. Meade would skillfully use his interior line to hold the strategic high ground at Cemetery Hill.

evidently absorbed by a hard problem. But this simple, cold, serious soldier with his businesslike air did inspire confidence. The officers and men, as much as was permitted, crowded around and looked up to him with curious eyes, and then turned away, not enthusiastic, but clearly satisfied.

After glancing around, Meade simply remarked, "Well, we may fight it out here just as well as anywhere else," and then rode away.

Union prisoner Justus Silliman had a close-up view of the Rebel activity in Gettysburg that day. He wrote afterward,

> The rebels had thousands of muskets which they had captured from us the day previous, collected in stacks in the street. . . . The rebels seemed to be having a good time generally and their rail fence gait told of empty whiskey barrels. They appeared perfectly happy and inclined to treat everybody with attention.

Silliman had been moved to another hospital near the German Reformed Church on the east side of town, on the corner of High and Stratton Streets. There he became disgusted with his own surgeons:

> Nurses were not abundant and I have done what I could to relieve the suffering. Several of our own surgeons are in attendence but to their shame are more neglectful to our wounded than were the rebel doctors. They will remain for hours at the windows watching the progress of the battle while our wounded were in agony for want of proper attention. We are in full view of the battlefield, the rebel line of battle being within a few rods in front of our hospital. Our own line is also in full view, they occupy a line of hills which they have fortified.

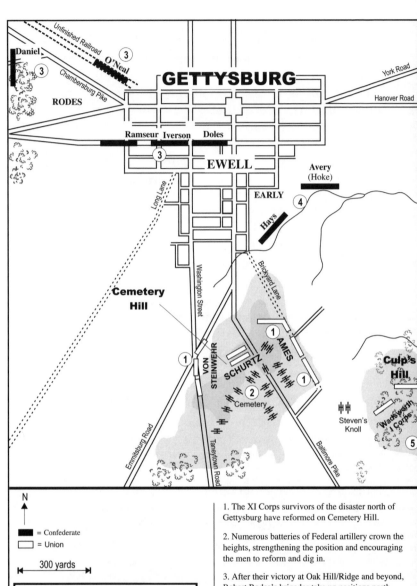

Troop Positions
at Gettysburg

Morning, July 2, 1863

N

= Confederate
= Union

300 yards

1. The XI Corps survivors of the disaster north of Gettysburg have reformed on Cemetery Hill.

2. Numerous batteries of Federal artillery crown the heights, strengthening the position and encouraging the men to reform and dig in.

3. After their victory at Oak Hill/Ridge and beyond, Robert Rodes's brigades take up positions northwest of town and inside Gettysburg itself.

4. Two of Jubal Early's three brigades deploy southeast of town, within range of XI Corps skirmishers.

5. East of Cemetary Hill on Culp's Hill, remnants of I Corps takes up position with XII Corps troops.

To be in position for the planned daylight demonstration, Harry T. Hays had moved his brigade of Louisiana Tigers forward before daylight into an open field between Gettysburg and Cemetery Hill near the red brick farm-house of William Culp. Positioned along Winebrenner's Run, the Tigers were behind a sheltering ridge that was about 600 yards from Cemetery Hill. Avery's brigade of North Carolina Tarheels took up a position on Hays's left. With the dawn came a very heavy fire from Union sharp-shooters on Cemetery Hill, who were armed with scoped Whitworth rifles. After learning that Longstreet's attack had been postponed, Ewell wanted to withdraw Hays and Avery but could not without exposing the men to a mur-derous fire. "So we had to remain there," remembered Captain Seymour,

> more than five hundred yards in advance of Ewell's main line of battle—hugging the ground behind a very low ridge which only partially covered us from the enemy's fire. It was almost certain death for a man to stand upright and we lost during the day forty-five men in killed and wounded from the fire of the enemy's sharpshooters. . . .

Lieutenant Jackson's and another company were ad-vanced even farther and served as skirmishers behind a plank fence. Jackson wrote after the battle, "and there we had to stay—if any one shewed themselves or a hat was seen above the fence a volley was poured into us."

On the opposing side, skirmishers from the 153rd Pennsylvania received a heavy fire from Hays's Tigers posted around the brickyard, on the east side of Brickyard Lane, and in houses and behind barricades on Baltimore Street. In town, the Tigers greatly annoyed the Yankees by placing hats on sticks, which they would raise up to draw their fire, and then let loose a volley of musketry when the Federals revealed their position. Unable to dislodge the

Rebels, Lieutenant J. Clyde Miller asked for help from the batteries atop Cemetery Hill. A few well-placed shells allowed the Federals to advance to a new position from which they could better see other Tigers positioned behind the ridge near the Culp house.

From his hospital, prisoner Justus Silliman watched the sharpshooters at work. He wrote,

> The La brigade were in a hollow in front of us, where they lay close until nearly dark though they had their skirmishers out nearly all day. These were occasionally picked off by our sharpshooters. Bullets frequently whistled around our hospital but I have not heard of any one being injured by them.

Skirmishing also took place between Avery's Tarheels and Adelbert Ames's division. One North Carolina sharpshooter severely wounded artillery Captain Greenleaf Stevens through both legs that afternoon, and Avery and two of his officers lay under a heavy fire behind the ridge bordering Winebrenner's Run. Avery's aide, Lieutenant John A. McPherson, remembered, "the enemy sharpshooters kept us uneasy all the time balls hissing all around us." McPherson observed that Avery had always remarked that if he had to be killed, he wanted to fall in a great battle. The randomness of sharpshooter fire must have been unnerving.

On the Union side, Private Mesnard of the 55th Ohio also suffered miserably while crouching behind a stone wall at the base of Cemetery Hill along the Emmitsburg Road (modern-day Steinwehr Avenue). He wrote, "At daylight the next morning the skirmish lines were hotly engaged, the wounded dropping out quite rapidly, and soon came back 'pell mell' over the wall. . . . A wounded 1st Sergeant from the skirmish line says, 'No one can stay out there under that cross fire. . . .'" Mesnard's company, nonetheless, was ordered out front. He recalled:

... and we were out there in a jiffy, but my how the lead did fly. ... As I was kneeling in the grass capping my gun a ball from the right struck my gunstock, stinging my little finger, and bruising my knee severely, and spoiling my gun. I picked up another gun, and suggested to [Lieutenant] Boalt that we charge on the post and rail fence behind which the rebs were, as I thought they were too close. The word was given and we got there. There was wheat standing on the other side of the fence. I raised up behind a post to look over as a bullet struck the edge of the post and glanced past my ear, sending splinters into my forehead.

Skirmishing and probes continued throughout the afternoon in the part of town nearest Cemetery Hill. Lieutenant Jackson's company, positioned behind the plank fence in advance of Hays's line, finally had enough. Jackson remembered, "While lying there late in the evening we concluded to back out of our position and go to the Regt. We had to crawl about 60 yds in the bushes then jump & run like '240' for about 30 yds. We all got into town & round to the regt. which had advanced and was posted behind a hill about 600 yds from the enemy."

Lee's final attack plan called for Ewell to use his entire corps to demonstrate against the high ground at Culp's and Cemetery Hills and to launch a full-scale attack if the opportunity arose. Johnson's division faced Culp's Hill, Early fronted Cemetery Hill from the north, and Rodes faced Cemetery Hill from the west. Early ordered Hays to command the assault against Cemetery Hill, using his Tigers and Avery's North Carolina brigade. For support, he brought Gordon's Georgia brigade up to the railroad east of town about a quarter of a mile behind the main line.

During the day, Johnson began selecting artillery positions from which to support the infantry attacks. He asked Major William Goldsborough of the 1st Maryland to reconnoiter

Benner's Hill as a possible artillery site. Goldsborough went to the top of the hill and found it to be completely bare and commanded by the Union batteries posted around the cemetery. When Johnson rode up, he shocked Goldsborough by ordering Lieutenant Colonel Snowden Andrews's battalion, which was temporarily commanded by Major Joseph Latimer, and Captain Archibald Graham's battery to set up on the exposed hilltop. Years later, Goldsborough wrote that he left the hill sickened at the knowledge of what was to come. Poor topography prevented Ewell from utilizing all of his approximately eighty guns, but by mid-afternoon, Latimer's sixteen cannons were positioned on Benner's Hill, while Ewell placed another sixteen on Seminary Ridge. On the opposing heights were forty Union cannons in superior firing positions ready to answer any challenge thrown their way.

When Longstreet attacked that afternoon at about 4:00 P.M., the Federals on Cemetery Hill could tell nothing of the action on their left except hear the roar of battle and watch the rising plumes of white smoke. They could, however, see the steady flow of Union reinforcements being pulled from nearby Culp's Hill and hurried south. Soon, a captain rushed up and excitedly told Schurz that the Confederates had broken through the left wing at the peach orchard and would soon be attacking Cemetery Hill from behind. The Federals spent several anxious moments until the sound of cheering on the left indicated that the Rebels had been halted and the danger was over.

Carrying out his orders to demonstrate against the high ground when Longstreet began his attack, Ewell's artillery opened fire at about 4:00 P.M. On Cemetery Hill, the Union artillerists were raked by the Rebel guns. One Northern correspondent in the cemetery wrote,

> Then came a storm of shot and shell; marble slabs were broken, iron fences shattered, horses disemboweled. The air was filled with wild, hideous

noises, the low buzz of round shot, the whizzing of elongated balls and the stunning explosion of shells overhead and all around.

One twenty-pound solid shot ripped through a line of Union soldiers lying behind a wall, killing and wounding a dozen men. Another Yankee claimed a Rebel shell exploded in the midst of one regiment and killed or wounded twenty-seven men. One Union officer wrote his mother of the destructive fire:

> One [man] had a piece of his head knocked off, all the flesh between his shoulder and neck taken away, and his right hand almost knocked off, he was still living when we left Gettysburg. He was a terrible sight when first struck, and when I had him carried to the rear, it almost turned my stomach, which is something that, as yet, has never been done. . . . I made one very narrow escape from a shell. One of the gunners, who saw the flash of one of the rebel guns, hallowed to me to "look out, one's coming," and I had just time to get behind a tree before the shell exploded within a foot of where I had been standing.

The Federal gunners gave as well as they received. Private Mesnard, positioned at the base of Cemetery Hill along the Emmitsburg Road, wrote, "Probably 30 to 50 guns on Cemetery Hill were firing over our heads. . . ." From his hospital, Silliman was exposed to the Union cannonading. He wrote the next day,

> At about four o'clock yesterday P.M. the fight was renewed with great fierceness. The cannonading and musketry firing was terrific and the sound of shells rushing through the air was continuous and resembled somewhat that of a tremendous waterfall.

Latimer's exposed position on Benner's Hill was pounded by enemy fire, but the young officer known as the "boy major" gamely held his ground. One soldier wrote that the hill "was simply a hell inferno," while another remembered "a continuous vibration like a severe storm raging in the elements." Finally, after taking heavy losses for an hour and running low on ammunition, Latimer informed Johnson that he could not hold his position any longer—the first time in his career that he had to send such a note. Johnson authorized Latimer to remove all but four of his guns—those four would be needed to support the infantry attack on Culp's Hill. After ordering his other pieces from the hill, Latimer reopened the duel with his remaining four cannons and quickly was answered by the Union artillery. One shell exploded over the major's head, killing his horse and nearly severing Latimer's arm. He was pinned beneath the dead animal, but his men rushed to his side and painfully extracted him from beneath it. The popular officer was evacuated to Virginia but died from his wounds a month later on August 1.

One of the Confederate gunners on Benner's Hill wrote of the devastation among Latimer's guns:

> Never, before or after, did I see fifteen or twenty guns in such a condition of wreck and destruction as this battalion was. It had been hurled backward, as it were, by the very weight and impact of metal from the position it had occupied on the crest of the little ridge . . . and such a scene as it presented—of dismounted and disabled carriages, splintered and crushed, ammunition chests exploded, limbers upset, wounded horses plunging and kicking, dashing out the brains of men tangled in the harness; while cannoneers with pistols were crawling around through the wreck shooting the struggling horses to save the lives of wounded men.

Hays's Tigers, positioned behind the ridge along Wine-brenner's Run, found themselves caught in the crossfire with a ringside seat at the duel. Captain Seymour wrote that it was

> a most exciting and thrilling spectacle. . . . The roar of the guns was continuous and deafening; the shot and shell could be seen tearing through the hostile batteries, dismounting guns, killing and wounding men and horses, while [occasionally] an ammunition chest would explode, sending a bright column of smoke up towards the heavens.

Everyone who witnessed the cannonade was impressed with its violence and remembered the opposing sides cheering when an enemy ammunition chest exploded. Confederate gunners claimed some of their bronze pieces became so overheated from the rapid fire that they were still hot to the touch an hour later. Latimer's sixteen guns fired an amazing 1,147 rounds in the space of a few hours.

After Longstreet began his attack, Ewell sent an aide up the cupola of the Catholic Church on High Street to see how the fight was progressing. (Ewell's wooden leg prevented him from making the climb). The aide reported

Major Joseph W. Latimer. Known as the "boy major" because of his youth, Latimer was one of the best artillerymen in the Confederate army. At Gettysburg, he was astonished when ordered to place his guns on the exposed top of Benner's Hill. Despite his misgivings, Latimer positioned his cannons as ordered and engaged in a fierce duel with the Federal artillery atop Cemetery Hill.

Longstreet was advancing and pushing back the enemy. Ewell then decided to make a real attack rather than just a demonstration against the Federal right. Johnson was ordered to attack Culp's Hill, and since he had the farthest to travel over rough terrain, he would advance first. When his attack began, Ewell would send Early and Rodes against Cemetery Hill and Cemetery Ridge, respectively. Ewell also sent a courier to A. P. Hill's left division on Rodes's right to seek cooperation, but he received no reply.

Johnson got into position during the artillery bombardment and attacked late in the afternoon. When the cannons finally fell silent, his attack could be heard roaring up the wooded slopes of Culp's Hill. Early then rode up to Hays's position along Winebrenner's Run. Captain Seymour remembered,

> Just before dark the solitary figure of old Gen. Early is seen emerging from one of the streets of the town and, riding slowly across the field in the direction of our position, the little puffs of dust that arise from around his horse's feet show that the Federal sharpshooters are paying him the compliment of their special attention.

Ignoring the bullets, Early sauntered up to Hays and asked if he was ready. Receiving an affirmative reply, Early then ordered the two brigades forward to seize the heights.

Hays had no delusions about the difficult job ahead. His men had always appreciated the fact that he never deceived them when it came to a dangerous assignment. Now, with the time at hand, Hays galloped along the Tigers' line to steel the men for the work ahead, shouting that Early said they must silence the artillery on Cemetery Hill. As encouragement, he promised that Gordon would come up to reinforce them once they had taken the guns.

The positioning of Hays's regiments is not known for certain, but he probably had the 5th Louisiana on the far right,

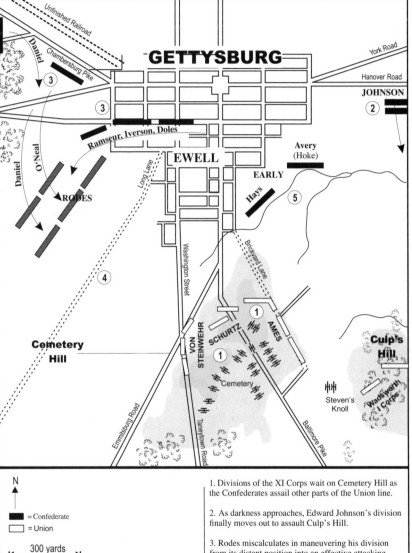

Ewell Prepares to Attack Cemetery Hill

Evening, July 2, 1863

Map labels:
- Unfinished Railroad
- Daniel
- Chambersburg Pike
- **GETTYSBURG**
- York Road
- Hanover Road
- **JOHNSON** ②
- ③
- ③
- Ramseur, Iverson, Doles
- O'Neal
- Daniel
- Long Lane
- **EWELL**
- Avery (Hoke)
- **EARLY**
- Hays
- ⑤
- ◄ RODES
- ④
- Washington Street
- Brickyard Lane
- **Cemetery Hill**
- VON STEINWEHR
- SCHURTZ
- AMES ①
- ①
- **Culp's Hill**
- Cemetery
- Steven's Knoll
- Wadsworth I Corps
- Emmitsburg Road
- Taneytown Road
- Baltimore Pike

Legend:
N
■ = Confederate
☐ = Union
300 yards

1. Divisions of the XI Corps wait on Cemetery Hill as the Confederates assail other parts of the Union line.

2. As darkness approaches, Edward Johnson's division finally moves out to assault Culp's Hill.

3. Rodes miscalculates in maneuvering his division from its distant position into an effective attacking deployment to strike the west side of Cemetery Hill while Early's brigades strike from the north and east.

4. Rodes's division clears the city and fully aligns itself here, along Long Lane.

5. Early's brigades prepare to launch their attack from southeast of Gettysburg, where they have been waiting much of the day for orders to move forward.

then the 6th, 9th, 7th, and 8th stretching to the left. Avery's Tarheels were on the Tigers' left, with the 6th North Carolina connecting to the 8th Louisiana, the 21st in the center, and the 57th on the far left, near Culp's Farm. These Tarheels were eager for the attack, having spent all day under a blistering sun suffering from the enemy sharpshooters.

After looking over the broken ground in their front, the North Carolina officers sent their horses to the rear, preferring to go in on foot so as not to draw attention to themselves. Colonel Avery at first decided to do the same, but then for some reason changed his mind and mounted up. He was the only mounted officer in the North Carolina brigade and perhaps the only one in the entire Confederate line. Hays launched his attack at dusk, with one officer remembering that it was a little after 6:00 P.M. Avery signaled his advance with a single bugle call from the 57th North Carolina, and many soldiers on both sides remembered years later how it wailed eerily over the darkening field.

Every Rebel knew the danger that lay on Cemetery Hill. Major Samuel Tate, of the 6th North Carolina, was no stranger to combat—he had already suffered one wound at Antietam and would suffer two more before war's end. He wrote, "Every man in the line knew what was before him." Captain Seymour remembered, "The quiet, solemn mien of our men showed plainly that they fully appreciated the desperate character of the undertaking, but on every face was most legibly written the firm determination to do or die." The 8th Louisiana's Lieutenant Jackson echoed his comrades' foreboding when he wrote afterward, "I felt as if my doom was sealed, and it was with great reluctance that I started my skirmishers forward."

Unknown to the Rebels, the Yankees on Cemetery Hill were not as strongly positioned as it first seemed, for Schurz had sent part of two brigades to reinforce Culp's Hill when Johnson attacked there. The cemetery was held by Ames's 1st Division, posted behind a stone wall that ran

A view of Gettysburg from the top of Cemetery Hill, looking over the Baltimore Pike.

along Brickyard Lane (modern-day Wainwright Avenue). This division had been badly shot up on the previous day and now was reduced to about 1,200 men.

Colonel Andrew L. Harris, of the 75th Ohio, had assumed command of Ames's brigade when Ames took over the division. Gettysburg was his first fight as a regimental commander, and now, on the battle's second day, he was leading the brigade. He had 750 men in the 17th Connecticut and the 25th, 75th, and 107th Ohio. The 107th Ohio was on the extreme left near the Baltimore Pike, with the 25th Ohio on its right extending a little northeastward to Brickyard Lane. There, the line turned ninety degrees to the southeast along the stone wall where Howard had deployed the 17th Connecticut the evening before. Down this wall were posted the 75th Ohio and 17th Connecticut (reinforcing the 17th Connecticut were about 300 stragglers from various regiments that Major Allen G. Brady had rounded up and put into line). Von Gilsa's brigade continued Harris's line to the right down the wall, with the 153rd Pennsylvania on the 17th Connecticut's right, and then the 68th and 54th New York.

Ames could expect help only from Schurz's 3rd Division—barely 1,500 men—posted behind a nearby stone wall just west of the Baltimore Pike. It could be called upon in an emergency, but not if Rodes's Confederate division threatened him from the west. The only other Union infantry in the immediate vicinity were von Gilsa's 41st New York and the 33rd Massachusetts (from the 2nd Division), which had been moved out as skirmishers beyond Brickyard Lane to a fence line on Culp's Farm. Ames sent them forward when the Rebel artillery barrage lifted, probably to strengthen the northeastern part of Cemetery Hill against Johnson's assault on Culp's Hill.

Besides the paucity of Federal infantry in the area, only four Union artillery batteries were able to bring the advancing Rebels under fire—Captain Michael Wiedrich's Battery I, 1st New York Light Artillery; Captain R. Bruce Ricketts's Batteries F and G, 1st Pennsylvania Light Artillery; Captain Gilbert H. Reynolds's Battery L, 1st New York Light Artillery; and Captain Greenleaf T. Stevens's 5th Battery, Maine Light Artillery. Wiedrich, Ricketts, and Reynolds were in position from left to right on the north-northeastern side of Cemetery Hill. Wiedrich was positioned nearly 200 yards behind the 107th Ohio, with Ricketts on his right, behind the 17th Connecticut and 153rd Pennsylvania. The battlefield's markers for these two batteries are in error. Instead of having six guns as indicated, Wiedrich only had four, and Ricketts had six, not ten. Reynolds was to the right of Ricketts, behind the 68th New York, and Stevens was approximately 400 yards southeast of Reynolds on a knoll between Cemetery and Culp's Hills. Although well placed, these four batteries were unable to see all of the Rebel line as it advanced.

Ricketts had been brought into position that afternoon and moved into a lunette that had previously been occu-

Union Colonel Charles S. Wainwright.

pied by another battery during the afternoon barrage. One of Ricketts's men was horrified to find a severed hand on top of the works and hastily buried it. After getting in place, Ricketts was approached by Colonel Charles Wainwright, commanding the I Corps artillery. The colonel ominously stated, "Captain, this is the key to our position on Cemetery Hill, and must be held, and in case you are charged here, you will not limber up under any circumstances, but fight your battery as long as you can."

It is not certain what particular route the Confederates followed in the attack from Winebrenner's Run, but Hays and Avery advanced over the ridge now occupied by a school. Hays then probably advanced almost parallel, and to the east of, Brickyard Lane for a couple of hundred yards, before swinging his line to the right, or southwest, to hit the Federals positioned behind the stone wall along the lane. Avery's North Carolinians, on Hays's left, advanced through the Culp Farm and orchard. The Tarheels advanced about 400 yards, swept aside the 41st New York and 33rd Massachusetts positioned beyond the orchard, and then wheeled to the right toward Brickyard Lane to stay connected to Hays's brigade.

The far right of the Union position, near Stevens's battery, looking north across the fields through which Avery's brigade attacked. Von Gilsa's brigade was positioned along Brickyard Lane, running along the tall trees in the upper left.

A Yankee who watched the advance from a distance said the Rebels started out from behind the ridge stooped over and disjointed, as if a mob had rushed forward. Then once under cover of the ridge, they reformed into a line of battle and quickly swept over it at the double quick with a Rebel yell. The Federals on Cemetery Hill were completely surprised when the Confederates popped into view over the ridge only seven hundred yards away.

The men in Stevens's battery had been listening to the fight roaring up Culp's Hill a quarter of a mile to their right. The sun had gone down by then, and the atmosphere was peaceful in their front. Suddenly, a sergeant jumped up and yelled, "Look! Look at those men!" as he pointed to the left around the Culp's Farm buildings. Glancing in that direction, the artillerymen could see Rebels climbing fences and forming a line. It was the Tarheels of Avery's brigade and the left wing of Hays's Tigers. Stevens quickly opened fire and was soon joined by the other batteries.

The 8th Louisiana's Lieutenant Jackson wrote that when Hays's line popped up over the ridge, the Yankee cannon "vomited forth a perfect storm of grape, canister, shrapnel, etc. But 'Old Harry' shouted forward! And on we went over fences, ditches and through marshy fields." In the growing darkness, most of the shells were poorly aimed and flew harmlessly overhead. Hays admitted afterward "we thus escaped what in the full light of day could have been nothing else than horrible slaughter." Captain Seymour agreed and wrote,

> The Yankees have anticipated this movement and now thirty pieces of cannon vomit forth a perfect storm of grape, canister, shrapnel, etc., while their infantry pour into us a close fire from their rifles. But we are too quick for them and are down in the valley in a trice, while the Yankee missiles are hissing, screaming & hurtling over our heads, doing but little damage.

This inaccurate Union fire also was verified by Silas Schuler, a member of the 107th Ohio. He wrote home that the "Artillery fired but they fired too high. Then we began to fire, but too high also." Unfortunately, the artillery fire also endangered some Union skirmishers out front. Lieutenant Milton Daniels, of the 17th Connecticut, wrote, "I remember the lead wadding from one shot killed one of our men, which demoralized us worse than the enemy in front."

Hays aimed his brigade at Wiedrich's battery, which had begun firing canister as soon as the Tigers swept over the ridge. Hays's right wing was closest to the battery and it charged. After the war, Colonel Harris wrote of the Rebels,

> They moved forward as steadily, amid this hail of
> shot shell and minie ball, as though they were on
> parade far removed from danger. It was a complete
> surprise to us. We did not expect this assault as
> bravely and rapidly made. In fact, we did not ex-
> pect any assault.

Another Yankee claimed the attack was "sudden and
violent." The right of Hays's line hit the 107th and 25th
Ohio, while Hays's center and left struck the main Federal
line along the stone wall. At about this time, Avery was
crossing Culp's Farm on Hays's left and realized the
Yankee artillery was far to his right. He quickly dressed
the line and then wheeled right to attack Ricketts's battery. Lieutenant Edward Whittier, of Stevens's battery,
later wrote that it was "a movement which none but the
steadiest veterans could execute under such circumstances." It first seemed to the Yankee artillerymen that
the Tarheels were heading for Culp's Hill, but then as
Avery made his adjustment, the line suddenly wheeled
right toward Cemetery Hill and charged straight for
them. Avery's left was the first to hit the stone wall, striking von Gilsa's position.

On the Union left, Harris's men fired steadily into the
Tigers as they ran for the wall. Lieutenant Daniels remembered how coolly two members of the 17th Connecticut
reacted.

> While the Tigers were coming across the meadow
> George [Woods] and Bill [Curtis] were sitting down
> behind the stone wall, and you would have sup-
> posed that they were shooting at a target. I saw
> George shoot, taking a dead rest, and heard him
> say, "He won't come any further, will he, Bill?"
> Then Bill shot, and said: "I got that fellow, George."
> And they kept it up that way, perfectly oblivious to
> danger themselves.

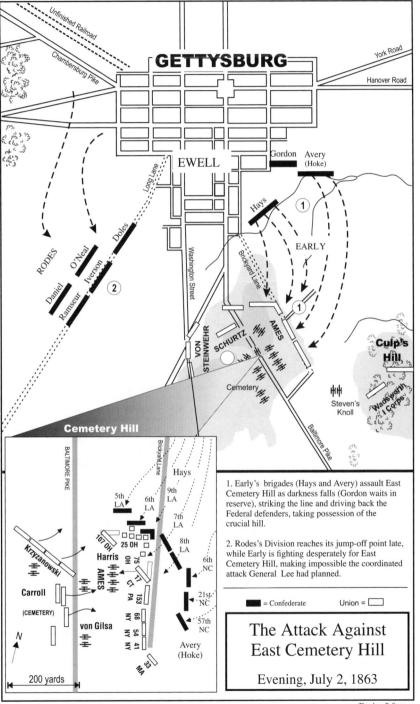

GETTYSBURG

Unfinished Railroad

Chambersburg Pike

York Road

Hanover Road

Gordon · Avery (Hoke)

EWELL

Hays

1

RODES

O'Neal · Doles

Daniel · Ramseur · Iverson

EARLY

2

1

Long Lane

Washington Street

Brickyard Lane

VON STEINWEHR

SCHURTZ

AMES

Cemetery

Steven's Knoll

Culp's Hill

Wadsworth I Corps

Baltimore Pike

Cemetery Hill

BALTIMORE PIKE

Brickyard Lane

Hays

5th LA · 6th LA · 9th LA · 7th LA

107 OH · 25 OH

Krzyzanowski

Harris · 75 OH · 8th LA

AMES · 17 CT · 6th NC

Carroll

153 PA

(CEMETERY)

von Gilsa · 68 NY · 54 NY · 41 NY · 21st NC

N

33 MA · 57th NC

Avery (Hoke)

200 yards

1. Early's brigades (Hays and Avery) assault East Cemetery Hill as darkness falls (Gordon waits in reserve), striking the line and driving back the Federal defenders, taking possession of the crucial hill.

2. Rodes's Division reaches its jump-off point late, while Early is fighting desperately for East Cemetery Hill, making impossible the coordinated attack General Lee had planned.

= Confederate ███   Union = ☐

The Attack Against East Cemetery Hill

Evening, July 2, 1863

Theodore P. Savas

Silas Schuler, a German in the 107th Ohio, wrote home of the charging Rebels, "They were all bent over as they charged up the hill." To Schuler's right, Lieutenant Oscar Ladley, of the 75th Ohio, was so awestruck by the attack that he estimated the enemy to number 10,000 strong. "They came on us about dark yelling like demons with fixed bayonets," he wrote home.

The thin Ohio line was stretched out in a single line, numbering no more than 500 men. Colonel Harris rode his horse up and down the wall shouting encouragements that the men must hold the line—all the while Wiedrich's cannons were firing shells over their heads. Sergeant Frederick Nussbaum, of the 107th Ohio, remembered, "Our orders were to shoot low, and we mowed the Tigers down as they came up the hill." Lieutenant Ladley echoed Nussbaum's account when he wrote, "We opened on them when they were about 500 yards off but still they came their officers & colors in advance. We lay behind a stone wall and received them with our bayonets."

The Tigers hit hard at the wall's angle and hand-to-hand fighting, described as "obstinate and bloody," broke out and spread down the Federal line from north to south. Schuler wrote,

> They kept coming up the hill right into the flat area in front of our position. Then we opened up our fire on them. Some of the fell. They came within about fifteen feet of our location. Our Adjutant asked their Captain, "Will you surrender?" "No, Sir!" So the Adjutant shot the Captain.

Lieutenant Ladley wrote,

> We lay behind a stone wall and received them with our bayonet. I was standing behind the wall when they came over. A Rebel officer made at me with a revolver with his colors by his side. I had no pistol

nothing but my sword. Just as I was getting ready to strike him one of our boys run him through the body so saved me. There was a good man[y] killed in that way. . . . I never saw such fighting in my life. It was a regular hand to hand fight.

During the struggle, a comrade behind Schuler stumbled and stuck him in the calf with his bayonet, taking Schuler out of the fight and to the hospital.

The fight along the wall was intense, and in the melee, the 107th's color-bearer, Sergeant Christian Taifel, was shot down when he waved his banner in the face of the enemy. Lieutenant Peter Young picked up the colors, however, and saved them from capture. Confederate Lieutenant Jackson admitted, "mr yank . . . did not want to leave. But with bayonets & clubbed guns we drove them back." Raising the Rebel Yell, Hays's men finally broke through the 25th Ohio's position. Sergeant George S. Clements recalled that the Tigers "put their big feet on the stone wall and went over like deer, over the heads of the whole regiment." With their line breached, the Yankees were forced to pull back to Wiedrich's battery so as not to be cut off.

The 75th Ohio and 17th Connecticut, to the right of the 107th Ohio, were in a stronger position, occupying a slight knoll that was somewhat elevated from the rest of the line. They opened fire on the Tigers at 150 yards and thinned the Rebel ranks. But the Tigers closed in and another wild hand-to-hand fight broke out, with one Connecticut captain actually grabbing a Louisianian and dragging him over the wall as a prisoner. These tough Buckeyes held the line, but to their left around the angle, the Rebels were streaming over the wall.

On the Union right, Colonel Avery's Tarheels still advanced successfully under artillery fire. While riding toward the wall, Avery was hit in the right side of the neck by a bullet and was knocked off his horse. In the smoke and confusion, no one noticed that he was down. Realizing he was mortally wounded, Avery took out a piece of paper and managed to scrawl a note to Major Samuel Tate before dying. "Major," it read, "tell my father I died with my face to the enemy." As he preferred, Avery had fallen in a great battle.

The 33rd Massachusetts had withdrawn to the far right when the Rebels first advanced out of Culp's Meadow, and Colonel Adin Underwood watched in the growing darkness as the North Carolinians moved forward. He wrote, "The roar and shriek of the shot and shell that ploughs through and through their ranks is appalling. The gaps close bravely up and still they advance. Canister cannot check them." The 57th North Carolina got within fifty yards of Underwood before his men opened fire. The Rebel line was staggered but kept on. The Massachusetts men braced for the impact, and the Tarheels' flag came almost within their position when Stevens's battery roared. The enemy colors fell, and when the smoke cleared the Tarheels were piled up in heaps. Above the groans of the dying rose a shout, "Good for Massachusetts!"

To the left of the Massachusetts boys, the Union defenders held a relatively low spot. Knolls and swales out front protected the Rebels until they popped into view only fifty to one hundred yards away. It was the perfect place for a breakthrough and there Colonel Archibald Godwin led part of his 57th North Carolina over the wall. As the colonel clambered over, a huge Yankee swung his musket, but Godwin parried the blow with his arm and hacked down with his sword, splitting the man's skull.

It was so dark by the time Godwin reached the wall that von Gilsa at first thought the approaching shadowy figures were Federals and ordered a cease fire. Shocked, a lieutenant in the 153rd Pennsylvania told the colonel that they were Rebels. As von Gilsa argued with him, another officer in the 153rd Pennsylvania ordered his company to fire. Von Gilsa immediately yelled to cease firing, but yet a third Pennsylvania officer cried out for his company to

From Cemetery Hill looking toward Gettysburg. The 107th Ohio was positioned behind the stone wall near the tall tree. To the far right is the German Reformed Church.

fire, as well. The shooting then became general, and von Gilsa finally was convinced that the line was, indeed, the enemy.

Staggered but not stopped, the Confederates rushed the wall. One Yankee claimed "clubs, knives, stones and fists— anything calculated to inflict death or pain was resorted to." A Confederate color-bearer, perhaps from the 6th North Carolina, carrying his flag in one hand and a rifle in the other, jumped up on the wall in front of the 153rd Pennsylvania and yelled down, "Surrender you Yankees!" A Pennsylvanian ran him through with a bayonet and fired into him at the same time. A witness remembered years later how the minié ball blew out the back of the soldier's uniform as it blasted through his body at point blank range. The Rebel fell off the wall, and the flag lay draped across the stones. A soldier from each side grabbed it, and a determined tug-of-war ensued until the Confederate finally was able to bring it back to his side of the wall.

The right center of the Federal line was held by the 68th and 54th New York, two regiments that were weak and nervous. Only months before at Chancellorsville, these same regiments had been flanked and routed by these very same Rebels. Only the day before, they had been flanked again at Gettysburg and had suffered terrible losses. Now, in the smokey twilight, the New Yorkers were hit hard by Hays's left wing and Avery's right. Sweeping over the wall, the North Carolinians killed the 54th New York's color-bearer and then wounded two men in quick succession who dared pick up the fallen flag. The New Yorkers soon fled back up the hill to Reynolds's battery about one hundred yards in the rear.

Most of Ames's line gave way in face of the onslaught except for the far right, where the 33rd Massachusetts and 41st New York stood firm, and in the center where the 75th Ohio and 17th Connecticut held. To cover the gap created by von Gilsa's retreat and to stem the flood of Rebels, the 17th Connecticut shifted down the wall to the right, stretching the line even thinner. The 75th Ohio's Lieutenant Ladley was disgusted at the retreat of von Gilsa's brigade. He wrote home, "They had driven back the dutch Brig on our right and had got behind us, and rebels & Yankees

Colonel Leopold von Gilsa. Von Gilsa was a profane former Prussian officer who immigrated to the U.S. and joined the Union. Put in command of a "Dutch" brigade, he was described by General Carl Schurz as "one of the bravest men and an uncommonly skillful officer." Despite his reputation, von Gilsa violated orders on the march to Gettysburg and was put under arrest. Fortunately, he was allowed to lead his men in the battle and played a key role in defending Cemetery Hill.

were mixed up generally. . . ." Sometime after the battle, he admitted, "I had a little revenge on the night that Earley's Div. of Ewell corps charged us, they [the "dutch"] commenced running back as usual. My sword was out and if I didn't welt them with it my name ain't O. D. L. It was the only good service it has done me yet, and if I live to see it home, I will have the satisfaction of knowing that if it never killed a reb it came mighty near laying out a dutchman!"

Ladley also bragged about his unit's stand. "The Ohio Brig swore they would not run and they did not," he declared. "We withstood a bayonet charge and drove the enemy back, and they were the best troupes the rebels had. It was Earley's Div. Composed of a Lousianna Brig and South [sic] Carolina Brig. They are called the La. Tigers."

Some witnesses mistakenly accused all of the Federals of running away after little resistance. Captain Ricketts later claimed this and accused the defenders of panicking and fleeing the wall without firing a shot, noting that many Union soldiers actually ran into the canister he was firing at the enemy. It was an ungracious comment, considering the resistance put up on the left by the 75th Ohio and 17th Connecticut. The smoke and darkness hid many brave acts; only those who fled were easily visible. In fact, the Rebels paid dearly for their success—particularly in color-bearers. When the 21st North Carolina lost its color-bearer, a major picked up the flag and was shot, then two more men were killed in rapid succession as they tried to retrieve the colors. "The hour was one of horror," remembered one soldier.

Generals Schurz and Howard were near the cemetery when they heard the shrill Rebel Yell as the Tigers charged the wall. Realizing instantly what was occurring, Schurz later recalled recognizing that the "fate of the battle might hang on the repulse of this attack." He ordered two of Krzyzanowski's regiments to fix bayonets and rush through the cemetery to help Wiedrich defend his battery. Along with his staff, Schurz rode toward the battle, as well, but encountered a crowd of retreating stragglers. Using the

Colonel Wladimir Krzyzanowski, whose two regiments were rushed to reinforce Wiedrich's battery during the attack.

flat of their swords, the officers began whacking the men to turn them back to the fighting. A similar scene was played out along the Baltimore Pike where some artillerymen blocked the paths of retreating soldiers. Grabbing fence rails, the cannoneers knocked down some soldiers and then stole food from their haversacks as they lay on the ground.

Cemetery Hill was the key to the Union line, and it now was precariously weak. Because some regiments had been shifted earlier from Cemetery Hill to reinforce Culp's Hill, only the artillery and ten undermanned infantry regiments were left to reinforce Ames. Thus, General Howard sent an appeal to Hancock for help, and Hancock responded by sending Colonel Samuel Carroll's II Corps brigade. Carroll was thirty-one years old and an 1856 West Point graduate. He had risen in rank from lieutenant to colonel in the first two years of war and had been wounded at Port Republic and Second Manassas. Called "brick top" by his men because of his red hair, Carroll had a vicious temper but was known to be a fighter and a dependable soldier. He had only three regiments available—the 14th Indiana, 4th Ohio, and the 7th West Virginia—but he rushed them

Colonel Samuel S. Carroll, known to his men as "brick top" for his red hair, had a temper but was a dependable officer. He rushed his three regiments through the cemetery after dark to reinforce Cemetery Hill.

through the cemetery so fast that soldiers had to discard their knapsacks and blankets just to keep up with him. By this time, it was pitch dark and so smokey that the men ran into headstones as they jogged through the cemetery. Some of the soldiers also remembered hearing the ominous sound of bullets splattering against the headstones as they passed through.

By now, the Confederates had lost all cohesion and were just two armed mobs rushing into the batteries—the Tigers on the Union left heading for Wiedrich's battery and the Tarheels on the Union right aiming for Ricketts's battery. Like water rushing around a rock, the Rebel line was split by the stubborn stand made by the 17th Connecticut and 75th Ohio. The 8th Louisiana's Lieutenant Jackson claimed it was so dark by the time the final rush was made, "we could'nt tell whether we were shooting our own men or not." Major Tate estimated only seventy-five of his men and maybe a dozen of the 9th Louisiana were still with him when he climbed over the wall, and Colonel Godwin reported that there was so much confusion in the smoke and darkness that only about fifty men were still with him for the final rush to the Union guns. Thus in all probability,

Alfred Waud's sketch of the Confederate assault on Ricketts's battery.

no more than 150 Rebels crossed over the wall on the Union right for the final charge to Ricketts's battery. One of those Tigers who accompanied the Tarheels was future general Leroy A. Stafford, colonel of the 9th Louisiana, who sprinted ahead to be the first to reach the guns. The fleet-footed Stafford, however, was passed up by his Major John Hodges, who was followed closely behind by the regiment's color-bearer, who defiantly jabbed the Tigers' colors next to a cannon.

Along the Emmitsburg Road, about 500 yards southwest of Wiedrich's battery, Private Mesnard's 55th Ohio also was forced to fall back from its position after it became caught in a crossfire. Hit in the arm, he ran back up Cemetery Hill and later recalled,

> The bullets seemed to come criss cross from every way, but I was just ahead of them. . . . As I ran up the hill between the cannon which were belching war, and on across Cemetery Hill I looked to my left

and saw the rebs right among our guns and noted through the smoke hand to hand fighting. . . . Dear me but that was a terrible place just at that time!

About that time, the wounded Mesnard encountered Krzyzanowski's reinforcements running toward Wiedrich's battery and claimed, "I came near being run over. . . ."

When General Schurz reached the batteries, he discovered "an indescribably scene of mêlée." Some Confederates were among the guns, and an intense hand-to-hand fight was raging, with the Federal gunners using rammers, fence rails, hand spikes, and rocks to knock down the enemy. From this point on, there is conflicting testimony about the fight for the guns. The Confederates claimed they captured the two batteries and held them for some time. The Federal artillerymen, however, said there was a brief, but fierce hand-to-hand fight at the battery, during which the Rebels entered the guns but remained only very briefly.

The Tarheels and Tigers captured the left guns of Ricketts's battery and tried to spike them with little success. A Confederate lieutenant grabbed for the battery's guidon on the lunette but was shot down by a pistol-wielding artilleryman who was nearby on horseback. The artilleryman then took the banner and turned to retreat, when he was hit by a bullet that tore through his body and shattered the flagstaff. Dismounting, the stricken man staggered to Captain Ricketts and cried, "Help me captain!" before collapsing dead.

As the Confederates tumbled into the battery, a Yankee lieutenant saw a Rebel point a rifle at one of his sergeants and demand his surrender. Quickly, the officer threw a rock into the Rebel's head, and the sergeant grabbed the man's rifle. As the Confederate fell, the sergeant shot him in the stomach and then began clubbing him with the rifle's butt, breaking his arm as he tried to parry the blow. The bloodied Rebel then cried for quarter. Later the lieutenant excused the sergeant's excessive zeal by noting that in the dark it was

Detail from "Repulse of the Louisiana Tigers" by Peter F. Rothermel.

not clear how badly he had hurt the Rebel with the gunshot, and the sergeant simply was not taking any chances.

While this bloody fight raged among Ricketts's left guns, incredibly the cannons on the right, only a few feet away, continued to fire. The battery lost six dead, fourteen wounded, and three missing during the close-quartered fight but continued to serve some of the guns. Afterward, a North Carolina officer acknowledged that Ricketts's artillerymen fought "with a tenacity never before displayed by them."

Meanwhile, many of the Ohioans on the left had fallen back behind Wiedrich's battery. One Rebel officer waved a sword and yelled, "This battery is ours!" but a German artilleryman declared, "No, dis battery is *unser*" and knocked him down with a sponge staff. Another Tiger officer threw himself across one of Wiedrich's guns and cried out, "I take command of this gun!" A German soldier holding the lanyard screamed out in German, "No you don't!" and touched off the piece, literally blowing the Rebel officer to bits. Private Arthur Duchamp, color-bearer of the 8th Louisiana, was wounded during the final rush to the guns, and Corporal Leon Gusman, a twenty-one-year-old former student, picked up the flag and entered the battery with a number of comrades. Lieutenant Jackson wrote after the battle that Gusman "was then wd or taken & our colors lost," but what actually transpired was much more dramatic.

When Gusman entered the battery, he waved his flag over the captured guns. Lieutenant Young, of the 107th Ohio, claimed the Rebels were "yelling like demons" around the cannons when Sergeant Nussbaum pointed out to him a Rebel, surrounded by a small group of men, waving a flag. Young ordered his Buckeyes to fire on the flag. Young Gusman fell to one knee, still clutcing his flag, and the other Tigers ran away. Young wrote:

> I ran forward, revolver in hand, shot down the rebel Color-bearer (8th La. Tiger Regt. as it proved by the inscription on the vile rag) and sprang for the colors, at the same time a rebel, seeing his comrade fall, sprang forward and caught them but fell to the ground, where I wrested them from him. These in one hand and revolver in the other, I was in the act of turning towards our men, when a rebel bullet pierced my *left lung and arm*. . . . I kept on my feet till I reached our men when all strength left me and my Sergt. Maj. Henry Brinker caught me in his arms as I was falling. . . . I learned subsequently that a rebel Lt. followed me with drawn sword and was about to strike me, when Lt. F[ernando] C. Suhrer

of our Regt. gave him a saber cut on the shoulder, which brought him down.

The capture of the Tigers' flag was a point of pride for the Buckeyes, and after the war different versions of the events emerged. At the dedication of a monument to Wiedrich's battery in 1889, Sergeant Frederick Smith stated, "One Rebel planted his colors on one of the lunettes of the first section (which was on the left), and demanded the surrender of the gun. He was promptly knocked down with a handspike, and the flag captured." This story is almost certainly faulty memory, however, for it insinuates that Wiedrich's men captured the flag. All other evidence clearly shows that the capture was made by the 107th Ohio.

Still another version of the incident came from Sergeant Nussbaum. He wrote:

> I noticed the color-bearer of the Eighth Louisiana Tigers waving his flag near the battery, and the color guards massing around on both sides of him. I called the attention of Adjutant Young to this demonstration, and there being about seven of us we at once, by command of the Adjutant, fired a volley and advanced toward them scattering the color-guards in every direction. The color-bearer being severely wounded, dropped on one knee holding to his flag with such a firm grip, that Adjutant Young who was trying to wrench it from him could not do it. The color-bearer had a large navy revolver in his right hand. I saw him pull the trigger and shoot the Adjutant through the shoulder blade; the Adjutant in turn planted his sabre in the color-bearer's breast. The color-bearer held on to the flag and sabre with a firm grip until he dropped over dead, never loosening his grasp until he drew his last breath.

We made a quick examination of the color-bearer's body and found seven bullet holes through him; we also examined the contents of his canteen which, being nearly full, contained whiskey and gun powder, and which we judged accounted for his desperate bravery. I took his knapsack which was a very neat one, made of leather with a goat-skin cover, and which contained a single biscuit lately baked being yet warm; being minus my own knapsack, I carried it a while, but the Comrades made so much fun of me that I threw it away for which act I have been sorry ever since.

The contradiction between Young's and Nussbaum's accounts on Young's wounding is curious. However, one must accept Young's version of his own wounding as the more accurate.

Maryland cavalryman Major Harry Gilmor, who rode with Hays's brigade, viewed another fight for a flag. In the twilight, he saw one of the Tigers' color-bearers climb on top of a gun and wave his flag defiantly before being shot off the tube. Then an Irishman grabbed the colors, yelled loudly, and mounted the gun. He, too, was shot off. Finally, a captain took the flag and climbed back on the bloody gun tube, but was shot in the arm that was holding the colors. Dropping his sword, he took the flag in his right hand and waved it proudly overhead. While giving three cheers, the captain was shot in the chest on his third cheer and fell off the gun. His men scooped him up and brought him back behind the wall, where Gilmor carried him back down the hill. By all testimony, the fight was particularly deadly for anyone who dared carry a Rebel flag.

Hays's Tigers had, for the moment, seized Wiedrich's battery, and Avery's Tarheels to the left had captured part of Ricketts's battery. Then in the dark, a strange quiet settled over the field, and the Confederates huddled around their captured guns and prepared for the coming counterattack.

Wartime sketch of Hays's attack from the Confederate side.

Out in the darkness the Tigers could hear the sound of massed men on the move and could occasionally see shadowy figures coming their way. Like von Gilsa earlier, Hays was not certain if the approaching men were the enemy. He had been told to expect Rodes's division to come up on his right and believed the ghostly figures could be it. When the Yankees were only twenty yards away, however, they fired three volleys into the battery, and Hays finally had his answer when he saw by the gun flashes that they were Yankees. He then ordered his men to fire, and the first Union line disappeared. In the gun flashes, Hays could see three more Union battle lines and realized he was hopelessly outnumbered. Outgunned and unsupported, he yelled for the Tigers to fall back to the stone wall, and a general withdrawal began.

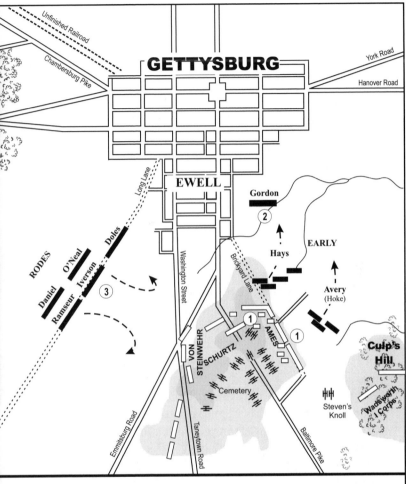

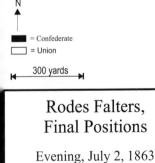

N

■ = Confederate
□ = Union

300 yards

Rodes Falters,
Final Positions

Evening, July 2, 1863

1. Federal reinforcements from von Steinwehr's XI Corps division, as well as II Corps men (Carroll's brigade), recover East Cemetery Hill and throw Early's attackers back down the slope.

2. John Gordon's fresh brigade waits for orders to support and exploit Early's stunning victory. They never arrive. His men do not fire a shot during some of Gettysburg's most dramatic and critical fighting.

3. Robert Rodes gets into position late and effectively turns over command to Ramseur, who advances and then, in conference with other generals, calls off the effort before contact is made. By that time it is too late anyway; Early's attack has already been beaten back.

The fighting on Cemetery Hill is over. The next day, July 3, General Lee assaults the center of the Federal position on Cemetery Ridge (known today as Pickett's Charge), but is beaten back, ending the battle.

Theodore P. Savas

The Federals approaching Hays were the two regiments sent by Schurz—the 119th and 58th New York of Colonel Wladimir Krzyzanowski's brigade. These two regiments had double quicked to Wiedrich's battery, drove the Tigers out of the battery with fixed bayonets, and then gave chase to the base of the hill while Wiedrich fired rounds over their heads at the retreating enemy.

The Tarheels on Hays's left also found themselves overwhelmed. The few men who had followed Major Tate into Ricketts's battery could hear Carroll's brigade massing out in the dark. Carroll's three regiments—14th Indiana, 7th West Virginia, and 4th Ohio—rushed from the cemetery into Ricketts's battery. As they approached, one of the artillerymen shouted, "Glory to God! We are saved!" The three regiments lined up to the right of the cemetery gate house and charged. Carroll wrote, "It being perfectly dark, and with no guide, I had to find the enemy's line entirely by their fire." Twice the Confederates dispersed the advancing Union counterattack with well aimed volleys, but finally they were forced to withdraw, as well, when they realized no help was coming. Unable to accomplish more, Major Tate ordered his men to make a run for it through the ever increasing hail of Yankee bullets.

Carroll sent his men rushing after Tate and captured a few of the slower Rebels. The pursuing Yankees then stopped at the stone wall at the base of the hill and blindly fired volleys into the darkness after the retreating enemy. No one fired back. Then out of the blackness came a deep Irish baritone identifying himself as a Federal and pleading for them to stop firing. When told to come over the wall, a large, burly Irishman climbed over and yelled, "Thank Jesus. I'm in the Union again!"

After Hays retreated, he was told that Gordon's brigade was coming up. Hays began reforming his line to make another try for the batteries and sent an officer back to find Gordon and to confirm that he actually was advancing. When this officer could not find Gordon, Hays went back

Edwin Forbes's illustration of Hays's attack from the Union side.

and found him waiting where the advance had begun at Winebrenner's Run. Realizing that Rodes had not advanced either and that it now was too late to make a second attempt on Cemetery Hill, Hays reluctantly gave up and brought his men back to a position alongside Gordon.

The failed attack had been costly for Early's division, which lost approximately 400 men, with Hays counting 181 casualties and the Tarheels 200. The Tigers were in a foul, disgusted mood when they returned and blamed Rodes for failing to support them. The men ranted that once again the Louisiana Tigers had breached the Yankee line, but others had failed to take advantage of it. One Yankee prisoner remembered, "A madder set of men I never saw. They cursed their officers in a way and manner that showed experience in the business. . . . It was simply fearful. . . . They said their officers didn't care how many were killed, and especially old Hays, who was receiving his share of the curses." A civilian who had watched the Tigers help rout the XI Corps the previous day wrote, "There seemed now to be an entire absence of that elation and boastfulness which they manifested when they entered the town on the evening of the first of July." From his hospital, Justus Silliman also witnessed the Tigers' return. He wrote,

> Just at dusk we saw those infalabile La tigers make preparations for a charge. They stealthily formed in line under cover of a hill and slowly and in excellent order advanced toward our lines till within a short distance of them when with a loud yell they rushed forward on the double quick. The clash was tremendous, but short, and Jackson's picked men retreated back panic stricken and with their ranks terribly thinned. Then in [sic] was that we were gladdened by the cheers of our men.

Colonel Godwin took command of the North Carolina brigade upon Avery's death and brought his surviving Tarheels back as well. Major Tate was furious that his 6th North Carolina had not been supported when it captured part of Ricketts's battery. When he found Godwin, he demanded to know why Godwin had not come to his regiment's aid. Godwin declared that in the dark and confusion, he never knew the regiment had made it to the battery. Unsatisfied, Tate eventually wrote a letter to Governor Zebulon Vance on the matter. He declared that while General Early would probably state in his report that the battery could not be taken, the 6th North Carolina had, indeed, captured it but was left without support.

CHAPTER 5

JULY 3, 1863

AFTER HAYS'S REPULSE ON THE night of July 2, Ewell decided only Johnson had a reasonable chance for success and heavily reinforced him with three brigades and two regiments. Ewell planned for Johnson to renew the attack on Culp's Hill at daylight, but the Federals attacked him first, striking Johnson at dawn on July 3, and indecisive fighting raged on the hill until Johnson finally withdrew about 11:00 A.M.

After Johnson broke off the fight, Ewell rode with engineer Major Henry B. Richardson to inspect his line to see if he could make an advance elsewhere. When he approached Hays's position in front of Cemetery Hill, the Tigers warned Ewell of the enemy sharpshooters who had been taking a heavy toll on the brigade. Ewell scoffed at the report and said they were "fully fifteen hundred yards distant, that they could not possibly shoot with accuracy at that distance," and "he would run the risk of being hit." He had not gone far when there was heard a thud, and Richardson reeled in his saddle, shot in the chest. A sharp whack followed when Ewell was struck in his wooden leg. Ewell helped Richardson from his horse and then quietly told an aide that he had been hit as well. When the frantic soldier asked where he was shot, Ewell showed him his wooden leg and stated, "I'll trouble you to hand me my other leg." Later, Ewell joked about the incident to

General Gordon. "Suppose that ball had struck you," he quipped, "we would have had the trouble of carrying you off the field, sir. You see how much better fixed for a fight I am than you are. It don't hurt a bit to be shot in a wooden leg."

Ewell finally sent orders for Early to attack Cemetery Hill again if he saw an opportunity, but Early decided against it. It is interesting to note that Ewell sent the same type of discretionary note to Early that Ewell had complained about receiving from Lee on the first day of battle. As it turned out, Cemetery Hill was spared further fighting, except another artillery bombardment that preceded Pickett's Charge that afternoon. In describing the shelling, General Schurz wrote, "The roar was so incessant and at times so deafening that when I wished to give an order to one of my officers I had to put my hands to my mouth as a speaking trumpet and shout my words into his ear." Although most of the rounds flew harmlessly overhead, the roar was demoralizing, and Schurz lit a cigar and leisurely walked around the hill to calm his jittery men. Although some damage was sustained during the bombardment, casualties were surprisingly light.

That night Lee met with Ewell and ordered him to withdraw to Seminary Ridge to shorten and straighten the line. Ewell did so, but he had to position his men on the field where the first day's battle had occurred. Captain Brown remembered the dead littering the ground. "Corpses so monstroulsy swollen," he wrote, "that the buttons were broken from the loose blouses & shirts, & the baggy pantaloons fitted like a skin—so blackened that the head looked like an immense cannon ball, the features being nearly obliterated—& that the necks were almost undistinguishable, being marked only by a sharp line between head & body. I saw one or two heads actually forced from the body by the swelling of both." Confederate artilleryman Robert Stiles wrote a similar description and reported that some bodies actually burst from the internal gases.

Not all of the Confederates made it back to Seminary Ridge. About daylight on July 4, Colonel Harris's Union brigade advanced from Cemetery Hill and recaptured Gettysburg and about 300 prisoners. Lieutenant Ladley wrote, "We went like a set of devils and raining as hard as it could pour down, and of all the waveing of handker-chiefs and smiling faces, you never saw the equal." When the Federals reached the Confederate hospital near the German Reformed Church, they found the guard asleep, captured him, and retrieved Justus Silliman and the other Union wounded being held there. Silliman reported that the Confederates had evacuated the town so quickly, they even left behind the thousands of captured rifles that had been stacked in the streets. He proudly reported home that "I have captured a La tiger belt plate also a piece of a reb flag. . . ."

Lee remained in position on Seminary Ridge throughout July 4 hoping Meade would attack, but Meade declined. Unable to accomplish more, Lee reluctantly began his re-treat to Virginia that night, with Ewell forming the rear-guard and leaving the field on July 5. The great battle was over. Gettysburg proved to be the largest battle of the Civil War and the largest ever fought in the Western Hemisphere. During the three days, Lee lost approximately 28,000 men, while Meade suffered around 23,000 casual-ties. Gettysburg would also be seen as a major turning point in the war since Lee's retreat coincided with Ulysses S. Grant's capture of the strategic town of Vicksburg, Mississippi, on July 4, 1863.

Gettysburg is sometimes referred to as the "High Water Mark of the Confederacy" because never again would Lee's Army of Northern Virginia have the strength it did that summer. However, that does not mean the Con-federacy was doomed. In hindsight, we recognize the sig-nificance of Gettysburg, but at the time it was just one more battle in a series of bloody encounters. Although battered, Lee's army was not broken. Captain Brown best summed up the Confederates' attitude when he wrote of the retreat, "It would be ridiculous to say that I did not feel whipped— or that there wasn't a man in that Army who didn't appreciate the position just as plainly. But the 'fight' wasn't out of the troops by any means—they felt that the position & not the enemy had out done us."

CHAPTER 6

CONCLUSION

EWELL'S FAILURE TO TAKE Cemetery Hill on the afternoon of July 1 is one of Gettysburg's many controversies. What has been particularly puzzling is how this supposed failure contradicts his excellent performance preceding the battle. Ewell led Lee's advance during the invasion; captured Winchester, Virginia; marched skillfully into Pennsylvania; and reached Gettysburg in a timely fashion to help rout the Union XI Corps. Ewell's stepson, Captain Campbell Brown, pointed out these impressive achievements to Union artillerist Henry Jackson Hunt in a postwar letter:

> The very brilliant character of Ewell's campaign, while in independent command—the capture of [Robert] Milroy's entire infantry, artillery and wagon trains at Winchester, almost without loss to us—the promptness, admirable discipline and dash of his advance on York and Harrisonburg—the precision and celerity with which the three divisions of his Corps were concentrated at Gettysburg—the vigor and success of his timely attack there. All seem to me to show high capacity for command. Not one oversight, not one error, not a lost horse, can be laid to Ewell's charge while in separate command. . . . Is it reasonable to suppose that one of the most active, zealous and intelligent of lieutenants, who had shown high military qualities up to that

time, should blunder and falter the moment he came under the eye of Gen. Lee?

Ewell's seemingly lackluster performance on July 1 is, indeed, odd when compared to his previous service. Understanding Ewell's actions is made even more difficult because most of the battle's written accounts were not recorded until many years afterward (after both Lee and Ewell were dead), and the participants involved in the controversy often directly contradicted each other.

The fact is that Ewell probably had little chance of seizing Cemetery Hill on the afternoon of July 1, 1863. A successful assault would have had to have been made very swiftly, probably before 5:00 P.M., or about two and a half hours before dark. What many armchair generals overlook is that, although driven from the field, the Union army was still intact and prepared to fight. Although the Confederates, and many Union soldiers, described the withdrawal through town as a rout, General Schurz disagreed. While admitting there was confusion and mixing of commands during the retreat, he claimed the Federals quickly reorganized after reaching Cemetery Hill. Private Luther Mesnard, of the 55th Ohio in von Steinwher's brigade, confirmed this. He wrote that he joined his regiment on Cemetery Hill just as the XI Corps was retreating before Ewell's assault and claimed his division of 4,000 men was already on the hill at that time. Hancock also had 4,000 men on nearby Culp's Hill and informed Meade at about 4:00 P.M. that he could hold the high ground until dark. Soon afterward, by 5:25 P.M., Henry Slocum's XII Corps was coming up and positioning on the right, and the divisons of Alpheus Williams and John Geary were both already on the field. Hancock would have had approximately 12,000 men and forty guns on hand, with the support of the approaching XII Corps' 9,000 men and four batteries. In addition, Buford's two cavalry brigades were near the peach orchard and could have been rushed forward if needed.

The Confederates were well aware of this imposing enemy force, for Captain Brown wrote, "By the time we got into town, the enemy had crowned the top of Cemetery Hill with a battery [of artillery] supported by quite a long line of infantry and opened on us." When they rode forward to reconnoiter the ground after entering town, Ewell and Early actually reported seeing at least forty guns on the hill. To make the assault, Ewell would have had only 6,000 to 7,000 men, not nearly enough to make the attempt a sure thing.

Although Ewell's failure became a great controversy after the battle, it was not a major issue at the time. Howard proclaimed to Meade on the night of July 1, "We could have held [Cemetery Hill] even if Lee had pressed his attack the evening before. . . ." Even after the war, General Schurz agreed with this assessment and wrote that the only realistic chance the Rebels had of capturing Cemetery Hill was if they had continued advancing while the I and XI Corps were tangled up in the streets of Gettysburg. The opportunity was lost, however, once the Federals occupied the hill itself. Schurz wrote, "It is therefore at least doubtful whether they could have easily captured Cemetery Hill before the arrival of heavy reinforcements on our side."

Schurz probably was correct. The only realistic opportunity the Confederates had to seize Cemetery and Culp's Hills that afternoon was to have never slowed their attack and swept right through town and up the slopes. This was an impossible feat, considering Ewell's confused ranks (having suffered 2,500 casualties); there being 5,000 prisoners to collect; sharpshooters to be rooted out of buildings; and sheer exhaustion, not to mention the erroneous report of Federals approaching the rear on the York Turnpike. To continue the push through town would have exposed the Confederates to devastating artillery and musketry fire from Cemetery Hill as they came down Washington and Baltimore Streets. The best chance for success would have been to move Rodes's and Early's divisions forward on either side of Gettysburg for about one and a half miles and then take advantage of protective ridges to get into an attack position beyond town. This would have been done in daylight under the watchful eyes of Hancock, giving him plenty of time to bring up additional troops. Historians may wield brigades and divisions with ease, but battlefield conditions and the "fog of war" make it much more difficult during the real thing.

Lee's orders and actions also caused Ewell much hesitation. The battle's first phase had taken on a life of its own, but it was over when the XI Corps was pushed back through town. Ewell then questioned whether making a second advance against the hill would violate his instructions not to bring on a general engagement, because it certainly would have required an all-out attack. Also, Lee was on the field by late afternoon and had A. P. Hill's men in sight. Since the commanding general took no steps to use Hill to seize the high ground, Ewell no doubt questioned the significance Lee put on the heights. Both Early and Rodes agreed with Ewell to postpone the attack until Johnson arrived, and Captain Brown wrote that they did so largely because they questioned the importance of such a movement since the troops under Lee's control were not advancing either.

The inaction of Lee has somewhat been ignored, largely because of a claim by his aide, Walter Taylor. In a postwar book, Taylor wrote that Lee sent him that afternoon to tell Ewell that Lee could see that the Yankees were disorganized and that Ewell only needed "to push those people" to drive them off the hills. Lee's orders were for Ewell to advance and take the high ground if possible. Taylor wrote that Ewell made no objections to these instructions and that he returned to Lee with the impression Ewell would advance. Taylor also claimed he later talked with Johnson, who said there was no reason why he could not have advanced and taken the hills, but that he had been ordered to halt.

Captain Brown absolutely refuted Taylor's claims. He wrote Hunt, "I say broadly that Col. Taylor's account of this battle is utterly worthless—that he carried no such order to Gen. Ewell and had no such conversation with Gen. Edward Johnson." Brown pointed out that Lee was with Hill not far from Ewell and his report stated he ordered Ewell to take the hills if practicable but to avoid a general engagement until the rest of the army arrived. This simple order is much different from Taylor's implying that Lee knew a slight push by Ewell would secure the hills. Also, Taylor leaves out of his account Lee's important caveat not to bring on a general engagement. "Is it credible," Brown wrote, "that Lee would if he attached the importance that Taylor seems to intimate, to the possession of Cemetery Hill, halt the troops under his own eyes & wait two or three hours in full sight of the troops of Ewell & Hill both, while the former was disobeying a vital order, without taking steps to have himself obeyed? NO—Taylor carried no such order. Ewell disobeyed none and evaded none. Is it not plain that if it was a mistake not to attempt Cemetery Hill that afternoon, the mistake was Lee's rather than Ewell's?"

Brown added that he knew Taylor would not intentionally lie about the events, but that time had simply muddled his memory.

Gettysburg can hardly be discussed without the matter being raised: What if Stonewall Jackson had been there? Many historians, and quite a number of soldiers at the time, opined that if Jackson had been leading the II Corps, the high ground would have been seized. Among others, Captain Seymour remembered a few years after the battle, "On this occasion I heard many officers and men exclaim, 'would Jackson were here.'"

These writers make two questionable assumptions, however. First, that the heights could actually have been taken with the available troops on hand, and second that Jackson would have made the effort. Assuming Jackson would have attacked, it is not certain he would have succeeded. Jackson was not invincible, and more than once he suffered setbacks by launching rash attacks. An assumption that he outnumbered the enemy led him to make hasty attacks at McDowell and Cedar Mountain. The first ended in defeat, and a victory was barely won in the latter. As for the second assumption, it depends on *which* Jackson would have been present at Gettysburg. Would it have been the swift and audacious Stonewall of the Shenandoah Valley Campaign or the slow and timid Stonewall of the Seven Days Campaign? Gettysburg followed two months of almost constant campaigning, just as did the Seven Days, and Jackson's poor performance in that campaign sometimes has been explained by fatigue. No doubt, Jackson would have been exhausted at Gettysburg, and he well may have curled up in some fence corner and gone to sleep after securing the town. The Battle of Fredericksburg also gives hints of Jackson's possible actions. There he convinced Lee to let him make a counterattack after repulsing the Federals. After inspecting the ground, however, Jackson decided against it because the enemy guns on Stafford Heights dominated the field. A similar inspection at Gettysburg would have shown that some forty Union guns on the hill controlled the area.

Not all of the Confederates who were at Gettysburg on the first day criticized Ewell's decision not to attack. One of Lee's owns aides agreed it would have been an unwise action. Colonel Armistead Long saw Cemetery Hill that afternoon and claimed, "I found Cemetery hill occupied by a considerable force. . . . In my opinion an attack at that time with the troops then at hand would have been hazardous and of very doubtful success." After the war, even Early agreed with Ewell's decision, although he was ready to attack on July 1, 1863. He wrote years afterward, "The question of the propriety of the advance was submitted to Ewell's judgment, and he did not think it prudent to make the attempt until the arrival of Johnson; and I must confess that, though my opinion at the time was different, subsequent developments have satisfied me that his decision was right." The truth is that Early's actions on July 1 are, perhaps, more questionable than Ewell's. He inexplicably kept half his division posted on the York Turnpike until the next day to guard against a flank attack that he emphatically believed did not exist.

Captain Brown perhaps best summed up the controversy over Ewell's failure to seize Cemetery Hill when he wrote, "The discovery that this lost us the battle is one of those frequently recurring but tardy strokes of military genius of which one knows long after the minute circumstances that rendered them at the time impracticable are forgotten—at least I heard nothing of it for months and months, & it was several years before any claim was put in by Early or his friends that HIS advice had been in favor of an attack & had been neglected."

A fair evaluation of Ewell was that he had performed credibly as a corps commander in his first large fight. He weighed all of the information available and decided to concentrate his force before rushing into an unknown situation. Time simply ran out before he could launch the attack. Ewell's biographer, Donald Pfanz, claims his real mistake was not Cemetery Hill, but in not forcing Early to seize Culp's Hill when Early said his men were too tired, and then in not keeping in touch with Johnson to make sure he had taken it as ordered.

Ewell never tried to defend himself publicly. Early later wrote, "He had, as I know, the means of vindicating himself, but the unselfishness of his character induced him to trust rather to time for his vindication than to incur the risk of a discussion that might in the slightest degree injure the cause in which he was enlisted." On one of the few occasions Ewell mentioned the controversy, he said, "Yes; I know I have been blamed by many for not having pressed my advantage the first day at Gettysburg. But, then, I cannot see why I should be censured. General Lee came upon

Brigadier General John B. Gordon. Gordon's Georgia brigade also was part of Early's division. On the first day, his men crushed the Union XI Corps' flank and sent it fleeing through Gettysburg. On the battle's second day, Gordon was to support Hays's attack on Cemetery Hill. This support proved critical to the battle's outcome.

the ground before I could have possibly done anything, and after surveying the enemy's position, he did not deem it advisable to attack until reenforced. Had I taken Johnson's fine division with me there would have been no second day at Gettysburg; but it reached me too late." Eventually, Ewell became more open and admitted to one man that "it took a dozen blunders to lose Gettysburg, and he had committed a good many of them."

Another controversy regarding the struggle for Gettysburg's high ground was whether or not Hays's twilight attack on July 2 could have changed the battle's outcome. Basically, two Confederate mistakes caused the dramatic attack to fail. First, Early had erred in not having Gordon immediately follow up Hays. From the edge of town, Early had watched as Hays moved his men forward and ordered Gordon to advance from the railroad. But by the time Gordon reached Winebrenner's Run, where Hays's assault began, wounded men already were returning from the front. They told Gordon that the attack was going well but that no one could see Rodes anywhere to the right. Realizing that Rodes had not moved up to support Hays, Early ordered Gordon to halt. Putting him into the fight without support on the right, Early believed, would have only added to the casualty list and gained no benefit. If Early had positioned Gordon closer to the front and sent him in immediately behind Hays, perhaps he could have reinforced Hays when the batteries were first taken and then held them against the Union counterattack.

The greatest mistake made by the Confederates that evening, however, was Rodes's failure to support the attack. As Hays and Avery advanced, Early sent a staff officer to hurry Rodes forward, but there was no coordination between the two divisions. Rodes, who was positioned inside Gettysburg, wrote that he had been ordered that afternoon to cooperate with Longstreet's attack on the far right as soon as an opportunity presented itself. When Longstreet advanced that afternoon, Rodes saw movement on top of Cemetery Hill and consulted Early. Both agreed to act together in an advance. Rodes began making preparations but found out too late that it would require considerable time to move his division out of town and get into position on Hays's right. Brigadier General Stephen Ramseur, whose brigade was to lead the attack, advanced his men and then crept forward in the dark to reconnoiter. Seeing a heavy line of enemy artillery and infantry, he reported the news to Rodes. By that time, Early's attack was over, and Rodes decided not to assault the strong Yankee position in his front.

It is not clear why Rodes did not move out of town earlier. Perhaps he wanted to shield his men from the Union artillery fire for as long as possible, maybe he simply underestimated the time it would take to get into position, or maybe he was just slow. The fact is that Rodes was an excellent officer, and this failure was out of character for him. It seems to be just another incident in the near total collapse of the Confederate command system at Gettysburg.

Early was very upset about Rodes's failure to support him and claimed in his report that he was forced to retreat from

Major General Robert Rodes. Rodes commanded Ewell's third division and was the first of the corps to see combat at Gettysburg. Although badly shot up while confronting the Union XI Corps on the first day, Rodes's division was to support Hays's twilight attack on Cemetery Hill on July 2. His slowness and lack of aggression seemed out of character for this usually dependable commander.

Cemetery Hill because of it. After the war, Early claimed Rodes's action was the greatest mistake committed by the II Corps at Gettysburg. This is a rather strong statement considering the controversy over the corps' failure to take the high ground on the first day of battle. Early may have simply been shifting attention away from his own failure to have Gordon positioned far enough in advance to support Hays properly. In his own report, Rodes said he had to move almost one mile to get into position, while Early had only to move a half mile. This was true, but Rodes did not explain why he did not start his movement earlier to make up for the additional distance. One possible explanation for Rodes's failure comes from Early's nephew, who claimed that Rodes was sick at Gettysburg and was in an ambulance much of the time. If this is true, it could be that illness affected his judgment and energy. If so, however, Ewell should have been aware of it and paid closer attention to his subordinate.

Ewell did not place any official blame on anyone in his report, only saying that Rodes did not advance. Captain Brown, however, wrote a few years after the war that both Early and Ewell thought Rodes had been too slow and that Ewell believed Rodes was to blame for the failed attack.

It is true that the II Corps' twilight attack on Cemetery Hill was poorly planned, and Ewell bears much of the responsibility for its failure. However, Ewell also has been criticized unfairly for not coordinating his attack with Longstreet in order to divert Union attention from their endangered left. The fact is that Lee never ordered Ewell to attack—his instructions were for him to make a demonstration and then turn it into an attack if there was an opportunity for success. Ewell did as instructed. He began the artillery barrage as a diversion when he heard Longstreet attack and then advanced late in the day when darkness helped cover his men. As it turned out, this proved to be the most opportune time because many of the Federals on both Cemetery and Culp's Hills had been sent south to help repulse Longstreet—only one brigade, in fact, was holding Culp's Hill. A more fair criticism of Ewell would be that he did not make sure that Rodes was ready to support Early when the attack was made.

The failed attack on Cemetery Hill on the evening of July 2, 1863, has not received the same attention as other aspects of the great battle. It should, however, because participants viewed it as a critical moment in the Union victory. General Schurz claimed, "The fate of the battle might have hinged on the repulse of the attack," and famed Confederate historian Douglas Southall Freeman wrote, "The whole of the three days' battle produced no more tragic might-have-been than this twilight engagement on the Confederate left." Even Private Mesnard wrote that Cemetery Hill was "the place where the battle of Gettysburg came nearer being lost than at any other point of time."

Could Hays have broken the Union line permanently if properly supported? And if he had, would that have given Lee the victory and the Confederates the chance to win the war? It seems that Hays could have been successful. If Rodes had moved out earlier, he could have been in a position to support the attack. Even if he did not break through the enemy's line on his front, Rodes's attack would have forced the Federals to keep Carroll's brigade in position and would have denied them the crucial reinforcements needed to drive the Rebels out of the batteries. Gordon then could have come to Hays's support, and Early would have seized the key to the Union right. While this does not mean Lee would have won the battle, perhaps there would not have been a Pickett's Charge the following day. All it does mean is that the Battle of Gettysburg would have progressed differently. We will never know if having been properly supported, Hays could have split the Union line atop Cemetery Hill and altered the war's outcome—it simply remains one of the Civil War's many "what ifs."

There is an interesting postscript on the struggle for Gettysburg's high ground. On December 8, 1941, Richard C. S. Drummond, secretary of the Cayuga County (New York) Historical Society, wrote Louisiana Governor Sam Houston Jones a letter informing him of the existence of what was claimed to be the battle flag that was captured from the 8th Louisiana atop Cemetery Hill. Drummond did not explain how a flag captured by an Ohio regiment had made its way to New York, but he stated that the last member of the local Grand Army of the Republic post had passed away and that the flag was found in the post's belongings. He sent Jones a photograph of the flag and offered to return it to the people of Louisiana. The flag itself was unusual, for it had a white background (instead of the normal red), a red St. Andrew's Cross (instead of blue), and the words "Louisiana Tigers" painted on it in blue letters. Because of its unusual coloring and lack of a unit designation, many historians doubt its authenticity. The point is now moot, however, for apparently World War II distracted authorities, and the banner was never returned to the bayou state. Recent attempts to relocate it have been fruitless, but perhaps somewhere in a dusty attic or old trunk there remains a relic of the bitter fighting for Gettysburg's high ground.

TOURING THE FIELD

Gettysburg National Military Park is located in south-central Pennsylvania at the town of Gettysburg, and it encompasses most of the actual battlefield. To visit it, drive north or south on US 15 to Gettysburg and follow the signs to the park's Visitor Center, located between Taneytown Road (State Route 134) and Steinwehr Avenue (Business Route 15). If traveling east or west, take US 30 to Gettysburg and turn south on Baltimore Street (Route 97) and follow the signs to Steinwehr Avenue (Business Route 15).

If traveling by air, the closest airport to the park is Harrisburg International Airport in Harrisburg, Pennsylvania. The next closest is the Baltimore–Washington International Airport near Baltimore, Maryland. The town of Gettysburg also has a small airfield for private airplanes.

The park's roads are open daily from 6:00 A.M. to 10:00 P.M., and the Visitor Center is open daily from 8:00 A.M. to 5:00 P.M. (to 6:00 A.M. in the summer). The Cyclorama Center is open daily from 9:00 A.M. to 5:00 P.M., and the National Cemetery is open daily from dawn to sunset. All of the park's buildings are closed on Thanksgiving, Christmas, and New Year's Day.

To tour the battlefield, one can acquire self-guided auto tour maps from the Visitor Center and Cyclorama Center or take walking tours guided by park personnel. Commercial bus tours also are available at several sites near the park around the intersection of Steinwehr Avenue and the Taneytown Road. There are also many licensed private guides in the area who can give a tour of the battlefield.

During the peak season of June through August, there are also numerous interpretive programs conducted by park personnel on the park's grounds.

Lodging is plentiful in the area. There are many motels and bed-and-breakfast facilities near the park that run the gamut from the privately owned, inexpensive, but comfortable, to national chain motels. Many of these are located along Steinwehr Avenue. There are also recreational vehicle parks along both Steinwehr Avenue and the Taneytown Road.

All of the sites associated with the struggle for Cemetery Hill are easily accessible. A good way to tour this part of the field is to drive north into Gettysburg along the Taneytown Road from US 15. You are now approaching the battlefield along the same road that much of Howard's XI Corps marched on the morning of July 1, 1863. Immediately after getting on the Taneytown Road, you will see Big Round Top and Little Round Top on your left. These two wooded hills played important roles in the battle, especially during Longstreet's attack on the second day. As you enter Gettysburg, you will drive over the top of Cemetery Hill, with the park's Visitor Center on your left and Evergreen Cemetery on the right.

To reach the area where the XI Corps' right flank was routed on the first day, take a right at the first traffic light, drive along Steinwehr Avenue to the next traffic light, and then turn left onto Baltimore Street. Drive north, go around Lincoln Square to Carlisle Street, and take it north out of town. Many Confederates, including Ewell, entered Gettysburg by way of Carlisle Street, while others came in on Washington Street, which is parallel and to the left. Turn right onto Barlow Avenue (you are now driving down the right flank of Howard's XI Corps) and park at Barlow Knoll. Here, there is a statue to General Barlow and several monuments for the 17th Connecticut, 153rd Pennsylvania, and the 25th and 75th Ohio. Nearby, was the Almshouse that became a prominent landmark during the first day of battle.

If you face north from this position, the Harrisburg Road is to your right.

On the afternoon of July 1, 1863, the extreme right flank of Howard's XI Corps was positioned directly in front of you in what is now woods at the bottom of the hill. Ewell's Confederate corps marched toward this position down the Harrisburg Road, with Gordon's brigade attacking directly toward you and Hays's brigade to the right along the Harrisburg Road. The Confederates drove back von Gilsa's and Ames's brigades, pushing them over Barlow's Knoll and back through Gettysburg. Ewell witnessed the fighting from atop Oak Ridge, which is the wooded ridge located to the northwest about a mile across the Carlisle (or Biglerville) Road. To view Ewell's attack route, return to your car, drive down Howard Avenue to the Harrisburg Road, and turn left. Just past Rock Creek is a school on the left. Gordon's brigade would have been advancing parallel to the road across the school grounds, while Hays's brigade attacked astride the road itself and to your right.

On the morning of July 2, heavy skirmishing occurred between the Confederates and the regiments of Orland Smith's brigade, which were posted near the base of Cemetery Hill between the Emmitsburg and Taneytown Roads. By walking from the Visitor Center north along the Taneytown Road (toward Steinwehr Avenue), you will cover the area where the fire was heaviest. On your left you will see a monument to the 136th New York and a plaque to Smith's Brigade, and farther along on the right (inside the gated cemetery grounds) is a monument to the 73rd Ohio.

Hays's and Avery's Confederate brigades were posted along Winebrenner's Run on the morning of July 2 and suffered from heavy sharpshooters' fire. To view this position, drive north along Baltimore Street and take a right at Middle Street. At the four-way stop, turn right along East Confederate Avenue and you will see a plaque to Hays's brigade on your left (farther down are plaques to Avery's and Gordon's brigades). The left flank of Hays's line probably rested about here, and the line stretched to the right to about Baltimore Street. Avery's brigade was posted on Hays's left and stretched the line farther down Winebrenner's Run onto the Culp farm. From this position, you can see the Culp farmhouse a few hundred yards to your left. During the attack on July 2, Avery's brigade advanced across Culp's orchard and meadow, located behind the house. Cemetery Hill is located about one-half mile away behind the school on your right. Notice the prominent ridge on which the school is positioned. This was the ridge that partly protected the Confederates from the Union fire coming from Cemetery Hill.

At dusk on July 2, Hays's and Avery's brigades attacked the batteries on Cemetery Hill from this position. They swept over the ridge in your front and then made a wheeling maneuver to the right. To get a better view of the ground, drive down East Confederate Avenue to the top of the hill and stop at the "Culp's Hill" marker on your right. This would have been about where Hays's left and Avery's right connected and at which point the wheeling movement was made to the right to strike Cemetery Hill. If facing the marker, Cemetery Hill is mostly hidden by woods, but it is located just to the left of the blue water tank. Colonel Avery probably was mortally wounded somewhere between this spot and Cemetery Hill. When you resume driving down East Confederate Avenue, off to the right, you can see the Evergreen Cemetery gatehouse atop Cemetery Hill in the distance.

To reach Cemetery Hill, continue driving down East Confederate Avenue. You are now driving along the position held by Johnson's Confederate division when it attacked Culp's Hill on the afternoon of July 2. Turn right at Spangler's Spring, follow the auto tour signs to Culp's Hill, and then park at Stevens Knoll. The statue to the left is to General Slocum. If you stand facing the "East Cemetery Hill" marker, you can see the cemetery gatehouse about a quarter of a mile away in the eleven-o'clock position. Directly in front of you, about a quarter of a mile, are located Ricketts's and Wiedrich's batteries atop Cemetery Hill. In the one-o'clock position, at the bottom of the hill, you can see Brickyard Lane (now called Wainwright Avenue). Von Gilsa's and Harris's Union brigades were posted along this road, behind the stone wall. Their line extended into the woods at the far end of the road, and there it made a ninety-degree turn to the left. The Confederates began their attack from the two-o'clock position, out of sight behind the intervening ridge. From this position, you can imagine the surprise of Stephens's artillerymen when they saw the Rebel line suddenly appear over the ridge top and head for them.

Follow Slocum Avenue to the Baltimore Pike, turn right, and park on the street near the gatehouse (or return to the Visitor Center and walk through the cemetery to the gatehouse). Walk down the path beside Hancock's statue and you will be on top of Cemetery Hill. Scattered around the area are monuments to Carroll's brigade, the 14th Indiana, Ricketts's and Wiedrich's batteries, 7th West Virginia, XI Corps, 134th New York, 73rd Pennsylvania, a statue of Howard, and a monument showing Howard's headquarters. The cannons located behind Hancock's statue mark Ricketts's position; those farther down the path mark Wiedrich's. If you stand in front of the "Attack on Cemetery Hill" marker, the school grounds behind which the Confederates massed for their attack are straight in front of you about a half mile away (beyond the trees). Hays and Avery advanced from your left to right over the ridge and then wheeled right to attack directly at this position.

Walk to the left to the stone fence and down the hill to Wainwright Avenue. The monument to the 25th Ohio marks where the original stone wall angled to the west. The 25th Ohio was posted from about this position to the west, and the 107th Ohio was on its left farther to the west. About twenty-five yards behind the monument, in the trees, you will find markers near the old original stone wall showing the right flank position of the 25th Ohio and the left flank position of the 75th Ohio. Walking south along Wainwright Avenue, the stone wall is missing part of the way, and the trees on your left probably were not there during the battle. Along the road you will see monuments, plaques, and flank markers for the 17th Connecticut, 54th New York, 7th West Virginia, 68th New York, von Gilsa's brigade, 153rd Pennsylvania, 41st New York, and 14th Indiana. The 7th West Virginia and 14th Indiana were not positioned here during the initial attack, but were brought up during the counterattack. Notice that the left part of the Union line (107th Ohio, 25th Ohio, 75th Ohio, and 17th Connecticut of Harris's brigade) were out of sight of Wiedrich's battery on top of the hill, which allowed Wiedrich to fire over their heads. However, on the right at von Gilsa's position, the Federals were in full view of Ricketts's battery, and some retreating Federals actually ran into its fire. Also notice the knoll in front of the position held by the 153rd Pennsylvania that hid the attacking Rebels from view until the last moment. Up the slope behind the marker for the 41st New York, you also can see the cannons of Reynolds's battery.

Two sites connected with the struggle for Cemetery Hill are located in Gettysburg. From Steinwehr Avenue, drive north on Baltimore Street to High Street. If you turn left, you will see St. Francis Xavier Catholic Church on the right. Ewell learned of the progress of Longstreet's attack on July 2 by sending a man up into the church cupola to watch the fight. If you turn right from Baltimore Street onto High Street, you will see the Trinity United Church of Christ on the left at the intersection of High and Stratton Streets. During the battle, this was the German Reformed Church, at which the wounded Justus Silliman was held prisoner in a Confederate hospital.

Return to Baltimore Street and drive north to Lincoln Circle. Ewell's headquarters were located in a barn north of Lincoln Circle near the intersection of Carlisle Street and

East Lincoln Avenue. At Lincoln Circle, turn right onto York Street. At the second traffic light, the street forks. The left fork is US 30, or the old York Turnpike, on which it was rumored that Union forces were moving into Ewell's rear on July 1, 1863. Keep driving straight onto Hanover Street (or Route 116), cross Rock Creek, turn right at the top of the hill, and park at the "Benner's Hill" marker on the right. This marks the position where Latimer's Confederate cannons were pounded during the artillery barrage on the afternoon of July 2. If you face the marker, Culp's Hill is the tall, wooded hill to the left with the observatory. To the right of it, you can see Cemetery Hill, the smaller wooded hill just to the left of the blue water tower.

This tour covers the major areas involved in the fight for Cemetery Hill. To visit other parts of the battlefield, you can acquire the park's brochure, which includes a detailed map for driving the park.

SUGGESTED READING

There have been more books written on the Battle of Gettysburg than any other Civil War topic, and keeping up with the literature can be a daunting task. A good starting place to learn about the battle is Edwin B. Coddington, *The Gettysburg Campaign: A Study in Command* (New York: Charles Scribner's Sons, 1968) and Mark Grimsley and Brooks D. Simpson, *Gettysburg: A Battlefield Guide* (Lincoln: University of Nebraska Press, 1999). Both of these cover the campaign in detail, and the latter has very useful information on how to tour the battlefield.

For a more specific study of Cemetery Hill and how it fit into the struggle, one should read Harry W. Pfanz, *Gettysburg: Culp's Hill & Cemetery Hill* (Chapel Hill: University of North Carolina Press, 1993) and *Gettysburg: The First Day* (Chapel Hill: University of North Carolina Press, 2001). Another excellent book that explores the controversial role Lieutenant General Richard S. Ewell played at Cemetery Hill is Donald C. Pfanz, *Richard S. Ewell: A Soldier's Life* (Chapel Hill: University of North Carolina Press, 1998).

The Confederate attack on Cemetery Hill on July 2, 1863, was a dramatic event and has been covered in detail by a number of studies. Among the better secondary sources are Terry L. Jones, *Lee's Tigers: The Louisiana Infantry in the Army of Northern Virginia* (Baton Rouge: Louisiana State University Press, 1987) and "Twice Lost: The 8th Louisiana Volunteers' Battle Flag at Gettysburg," *Civil War Regiments*, Vol. 6, No. 3; Charles P. Hamblen, *Connecticut Yankees at Gettysburg*, edited by Walter L. Powell (Kent: Kent State University Press, 1993); and Peter Tomasak, "'Glory to God! We Are Saved!' Night Assault at Gettysburg," *North & South*, Vol. 1, No. 5.

Some of the best sources on the fight for Cemetery Hill are the accounts left by the soldiers themselves. Two of the greatest collections of first person accounts are the U.S. War Department, *The War of the Rebellion: A Compilation of the Official Records of the Union and Confederate Armies*, 128 vols. (Washington, D.C.: U.S. Government Printing Office, 1880–1901) and David L. Ladd and Audrey J. Ladd, eds., *The Bachelder Papers: Gettysburg in Their Own Words* (Dayton: Morningside, 1994). The former is the official government publication of Civil War military records, including the officers' battle reports, with volume 27 covering the Battle of Gettysburg. The latter is a large collection of first person accounts on the battle that were compiled after the war. The *Southern Historical Society Papers* also contain numerous first-person accounts of the struggle and are particularly useful in studying the controversial Confederate decisions made at Gettysburg.

There also have been published many soldiers' memoirs and letters. Among the useful ones that cover the Union side of the struggle for Cemetery Hill are William T. Parsons and Mary Shuler Heimburger, "Shuler Family Correspondence," *Pennsylvania Folklife*, Vol. 29 (Spring 1980); Robert Hoffsommer, ed., "The Rise and Survival of Private Mesnard," *Civil War Times Illustrated* (February 1986); Carl M. Becker and Ritchie Thomas, eds., *Hearth and Knapsack: The Ladley Letters, 1857–1880* (Athens: Ohio University Press, 1988); Edward Marcus, ed., *A New Canaan Private in the Civil War: Letters of Justus M. Silliman, 17th Connecticut Volunteers* (New Canaan, Conn.: New Canaan Historical Society, 1984); Austin C. Stearns, *Three Years with Company K*, edited by Arthur A. Kent (London, 1976); Oliver O. Howard, *Autobiography of Oliver Otis Howard*, 2 vols. (New York: Baker and Taylor Company, 1902); Carl Schurz, *The Reminiscences of Carl Schurz*, 3 vols. (New York:

McClure Company, 1907–08); Almira Hancock, *Reminiscences of Winfield Scott Hancock* (New York: Charles L. Webster & Company, 1887); and Jacob Smith, *Camps and Campaigns of the 107th Ohio Volunteer Infantry* (n.p., n.d).

Published accounts by the Confederates include Walter H. Taylor, *Four Years With General Lee*, edited by James I. Robertson (New York: Bonanza Books, 1962); Jubal A. Early, *Autobiographical Sketch and Narrative of the War between the States* (Philadelphia: Lippincott, 1912); and Terry L. Jones, ed., *Campbell Brown's Civil War: With Ewell and the Army of Northern Virginia* (Baton Rouge: Louisiana State University Press, 2001), *The Civil War Memoirs of Capt. William J. Seymour: Reminiscences of a Louisiana Tiger* (Baton Rouge: Louisiana State University Press, 1991), and "Going Back into the Union at Last," *Civil War Times Illustrated* (January-February 1991).

INDEX

Index